50 Cocktail Party Bite Recipes for Home

By: Kelly Johnson

Table of Contents

- Mini Caprese Skewers
- Bacon-Wrapped Dates
- Spinach Artichoke Dip Bites
- Bruschetta with Tomato and Basil
- Teriyaki Chicken Meatballs
- Smoked Salmon Canapés
- Stuffed Mushrooms
- Mini Chicken Quesadillas
- Pesto Tortellini Skewers
- Coconut Shrimp
- Prosciutto-Wrapped Melon
- Crab Cakes
- Mini Reuben Sandwiches
- Spanakopita Triangles
- Antipasto Skewers
- Buffalo Cauliflower Bites
- Meatball Sliders
- Phyllo-Wrapped Asparagus
- Mini Quiche
- Deviled Eggs
- Teriyaki Beef Skewers
- Cucumber Smoked Salmon Rolls
- Chicken Satay Skewers
- Stuffed Cherry Tomatoes
- Jalapeño Poppers
- Greek Yogurt Dip with Veggie Sticks
- Crab Stuffed Mushrooms
- Thai Lettuce Wraps
- Caprese Salad Bites
- Mini Beef Wellingtons
- BBQ Chicken Sliders
- Sweet Potato Rounds with Goat Cheese
- Buffalo Chicken Dip Cups
- Mini Tacos
- Ratatouille Tartlets

- Coconut Chicken Tenders
- Tomato Basil Bruschetta
- Buffalo Cauliflower Bites
- Vietnamese Spring Rolls
- Greek Meatballs
- Pimento Cheese Stuffed Peppers
- Chicken Wonton Cups
- Polenta Bites with Pesto and Tomato
- Zucchini Fritters
- Mushroom Puff Pastry Bites
- Avocado Shrimp Ceviche
- Teriyaki Salmon Skewers
- Mini Crab Tarts
- Puff Pastry Pinwheels
- Olive and Cheese Skewers

Mini Caprese Skewers

Ingredients:

- Cherry or grape tomatoes
- Fresh mini mozzarella balls (bocconcini)
- Fresh basil leaves
- Balsamic glaze or balsamic vinegar and olive oil (for drizzling)
- Salt and pepper (optional)

Instructions:

Prepare your cherry or grape tomatoes by washing and drying them.
Drain the mini mozzarella balls if they're stored in water or brine.
Wash and pat dry the fresh basil leaves.
To assemble each skewer, thread one cherry tomato, one mini mozzarella ball, and one basil leaf onto a toothpick or small skewer.
Repeat the process until you have assembled all your skewers.
Arrange the skewers on a serving platter or tray.
Just before serving, drizzle the skewers with balsamic glaze or a mixture of balsamic vinegar and olive oil.
Optionally, season with a sprinkle of salt and pepper to taste.
Serve immediately and enjoy these tasty Mini Caprese Skewers as a delightful appetizer for cocktail parties or gatherings.

Bacon-Wrapped Dates

Ingredients:

- Medjool dates, pitted
- Whole almonds or almond pieces (optional)
- Thinly sliced bacon, cut into thirds or halves depending on the size of your dates
- Toothpicks or cocktail sticks

Instructions:

Preheat your oven to 375°F (190°C).
If your dates are not already pitted, carefully make a slit along one side of each date and remove the pit. If desired, insert a whole almond or a piece of almond into each date in place of the pit.
Take a piece of bacon and wrap it around a date, covering as much of the date as possible. Secure the bacon with a toothpick or cocktail stick.

Place the bacon-wrapped dates on a baking sheet lined with parchment paper or aluminum foil to prevent sticking.

Repeat the process with the remaining dates and bacon slices.

Place the baking sheet in the preheated oven and bake for about 15-20 minutes, or until the bacon is crispy and golden brown.

Once cooked, remove the bacon-wrapped dates from the oven and let them cool slightly before serving.

Optionally, you can serve these bacon-wrapped dates warm or at room temperature. They make a fantastic sweet and savory appetizer for cocktail parties or any gathering.

Variations:

- Sweet and Spicy: Sprinkle the bacon-wrapped dates with brown sugar or a pinch of cayenne pepper before baking for a sweet and spicy kick.
- Cheese-Stuffed: Insert a small cube of cheese (such as goat cheese or blue cheese) into the pitted date before wrapping with bacon.
- Balsamic Glaze: Drizzle the baked bacon-wrapped dates with a balsamic reduction for an extra burst of flavor.

Enjoy these irresistible bacon-wrapped dates as a crowd-pleasing appetizer!

Spinach Artichoke Dip Bites

Ingredients:

- 1 package (10 oz) frozen chopped spinach, thawed and squeezed dry
- 1 can (14 oz) artichoke hearts, drained and finely chopped
- 1 cup shredded mozzarella cheese
- 1/2 cup grated Parmesan cheese
- 1/2 cup mayonnaise
- 1/2 cup sour cream
- 2 cloves garlic, minced
- Salt and pepper, to taste
- 2 tubes (8 oz each) refrigerated crescent roll dough
- Optional: Chopped fresh parsley or green onions for garnish

Instructions:

Preheat your oven to 375°F (190°C) and lightly grease mini muffin pans or baking sheets.

In a mixing bowl, combine the chopped spinach, chopped artichoke hearts, shredded mozzarella cheese, grated Parmesan cheese, mayonnaise, sour cream, minced garlic, salt, and pepper. Mix until well combined.

Roll out the crescent roll dough and separate into triangles along the perforated lines. Cut each triangle into smaller triangles or squares, depending on the size of your muffin pans or baking sheets.

Press each crescent roll triangle or square into the wells of the mini muffin pans or onto the baking sheets to form small cups.

Spoon the spinach artichoke mixture into each crescent roll cup, filling them nearly to the top.

Bake in the preheated oven for about 12-15 minutes or until the crescent roll cups are golden brown and the filling is bubbly and heated through.

Remove the spinach artichoke dip bites from the oven and let them cool slightly in the pans before transferring to a serving platter.

If desired, garnish with chopped fresh parsley or green onions before serving.

These spinach artichoke dip bites are perfect for parties, potlucks, or as a tasty appetizer for any occasion. Enjoy the creamy, cheesy goodness in every bite!

Bruschetta with Tomato and Basil

Ingredients:

- 1 French baguette, sliced into 1/2-inch thick slices
- 4-5 ripe tomatoes, diced
- 1/4 cup fresh basil leaves, chopped
- 2 cloves garlic, minced
- 2 tablespoons extra virgin olive oil, plus extra for drizzling
- 1 tablespoon balsamic vinegar (optional)
- Salt and freshly ground black pepper, to taste

Instructions:

Preheat your oven to 375°F (190°C). Arrange the baguette slices on a baking sheet in a single layer.
Drizzle the baguette slices lightly with olive oil. Place them in the preheated oven and toast for about 8-10 minutes, or until they are golden and crispy. Remove from the oven and set aside.
In a mixing bowl, combine the diced tomatoes, chopped basil, minced garlic, olive oil, and balsamic vinegar (if using). Season with salt and pepper to taste. Mix well to combine all the flavors.
Spoon the tomato and basil mixture generously onto each toasted baguette slice.
Drizzle a little extra olive oil over the bruschetta for added flavor and shine.
Arrange the bruschetta on a serving platter and serve immediately.

Enjoy this classic bruschetta with tomato and basil as a delicious appetizer or snack. It's perfect for parties, gatherings, or anytime you want to savor the flavors of fresh tomatoes and basil on crispy bread.

Teriyaki Chicken Meatballs

Ingredients:

- For the Meatballs:
    - 1 pound ground chicken
    - 1/2 cup breadcrumbs
    - 1/4 cup finely chopped green onions (scallions)
    - 1 large egg
    - 2 cloves garlic, minced
    - 1 tablespoon soy sauce
    - Salt and pepper, to taste
    - Sesame seeds, for garnish (optional)
- For the Teriyaki Sauce:
    - 1/2 cup soy sauce
    - 1/4 cup water
    - 2 tablespoons honey or brown sugar
    - 2 cloves garlic, minced
    - 1 teaspoon grated ginger (optional)
    - 1 tablespoon cornstarch mixed with 2 tablespoons water (to thicken)

Instructions:

Preheat Oven: Preheat your oven to 400°F (200°C) and line a baking sheet with parchment paper or foil.
Make the Meatballs:
- In a large mixing bowl, combine ground chicken, breadcrumbs, chopped green onions, egg, minced garlic, soy sauce, salt, and pepper. Mix until well combined.
- Shape the mixture into small meatballs, about 1 inch in diameter, and arrange them on the prepared baking sheet.

Bake the Meatballs:
- Bake the meatballs in the preheated oven for 15-20 minutes, or until cooked through and golden brown.

Make the Teriyaki Sauce:
- While the meatballs are baking, prepare the teriyaki sauce. In a small saucepan, combine soy sauce, water, honey or brown sugar, minced garlic, and grated ginger (if using). Bring to a simmer over medium heat.
- In a small bowl, mix the cornstarch with water to make a slurry. Gradually add the cornstarch slurry to the simmering sauce, stirring constantly, until the sauce thickens to your desired consistency. Remove from heat.

Combine Meatballs with Sauce:
- Once the meatballs are cooked, transfer them to a large bowl. Pour the prepared teriyaki sauce over the meatballs and gently toss to coat.

Serve:

- Arrange the teriyaki chicken meatballs on a serving platter. Sprinkle with sesame seeds for garnish, if desired.
- Serve hot as an appetizer with toothpicks or as a main dish with rice or noodles.

Enjoy these delicious teriyaki chicken meatballs as a crowd-pleasing appetizer at parties or as a tasty meal for dinner!

Smoked Salmon Canapés

Ingredients:

- For the Canapés:
    - Sliced French baguette or cocktail rye bread
    - Cream cheese or goat cheese
    - Smoked salmon slices
    - Fresh dill, chopped
    - Capers (optional)
    - Lemon wedges, for serving

Instructions:

Prepare the Bread:
- Slice the French baguette or cocktail rye bread into thin rounds. Alternatively, you can use pre-made mini toast rounds or crackers as a base for your canapés.

Spread the Cheese:
- Spread a thin layer of cream cheese or goat cheese onto each bread round. The cheese acts as a creamy base for the smoked salmon.

Add the Smoked Salmon:
- Cut the smoked salmon slices into smaller pieces to fit onto the bread rounds.
- Place a piece of smoked salmon on top of each bread round with cheese.

Garnish:
- Sprinkle chopped fresh dill over the smoked salmon canapés for a pop of flavor and color.
- Optionally, top each canapé with a few capers for a briny touch.

Serve:
- Arrange the smoked salmon canapés on a serving platter.
- Garnish the platter with lemon wedges for guests to squeeze over the canapés before enjoying.

Variations:

- Cucumber Base: Instead of bread rounds, use thinly sliced cucumber rounds as a base for your smoked salmon canapés.
- Herb Butter: Mix softened butter with chopped herbs like dill, chives, or parsley, and spread it on the bread rounds before adding the smoked salmon.
- Horseradish Cream: Add a kick of flavor by mixing some prepared horseradish into the cream cheese before spreading it on the bread.

These smoked salmon canapés are not only visually appealing but also bursting with flavor.

They make a sophisticated addition to any party spread and are sure to impress your guests!

Enjoy making and serving these delightful appetizers.

Stuffed Mushrooms

Ingredients:

- 12-16 large button or cremini mushrooms
- 1/2 cup Italian-style breadcrumbs
- 1/4 cup grated Parmesan cheese
- 2 cloves garlic, minced
- 2 tablespoons fresh parsley, chopped
- 3 tablespoons olive oil
- Salt and pepper, to taste
- Optional: Additional grated cheese for topping

Instructions:

Preheat Oven: Preheat your oven to 375°F (190°C). Lightly grease a baking dish or line it with parchment paper.
Prepare Mushrooms: Clean the mushrooms by wiping them with a damp paper towel to remove any dirt. Remove the stems from the mushrooms and finely chop them. Set aside.
Prepare Filling: In a bowl, combine the chopped mushroom stems, breadcrumbs, grated Parmesan cheese, minced garlic, chopped parsley, olive oil, salt, and pepper. Mix well to form a moist stuffing.
Stuff the Mushrooms: Spoon the filling mixture into the mushroom caps, pressing gently to pack the filling.
Bake: Arrange the stuffed mushrooms in the prepared baking dish. If desired, sprinkle additional grated cheese on top of each stuffed mushroom.
Bake in Oven: Bake the stuffed mushrooms in the preheated oven for 20-25 minutes, or until the mushrooms are tender and the filling is golden brown.
Serve: Remove the stuffed mushrooms from the oven and let them cool slightly before serving. Arrange them on a serving platter and garnish with fresh parsley if desired.

Variations:

- Creamy Filling: Add cream cheese, sour cream, or ricotta cheese to the filling mixture for a creamy texture.
- Meaty Option: Mix cooked and crumbled sausage or chopped bacon into the filling mixture for a heartier stuffed mushroom.

- Herb Infused: Experiment with different herbs such as thyme, oregano, or basil to customize the flavor of the stuffing.

These stuffed mushrooms are perfect for entertaining and can be easily customized based on your preferences. They make a tasty and satisfying appetizer that will disappear quickly from the party table!

Mini Chicken Quesadillas

Ingredients:

- 8 small flour tortillas (6-inch size)
- 1 cup cooked and shredded chicken (rotisserie chicken works well)
- 1 cup shredded cheese (cheddar, Monterey Jack, or a blend)
- 1/4 cup diced bell peppers (any color)
- 2 tablespoons chopped fresh cilantro (optional)
- 1/2 teaspoon chili powder
- 1/2 teaspoon cumin
- Salt and pepper, to taste
- Cooking spray or vegetable oil, for cooking

Optional Garnishes and Dipping Sauce:

- Salsa
- Guacamole
- Sour cream
- Chopped green onions
- Sliced jalapeños

Instructions:

Prepare the Filling: In a bowl, combine the shredded chicken, shredded cheese, diced bell peppers, chopped cilantro (if using), chili powder, cumin, salt, and pepper. Mix well to combine all the ingredients.

Assemble the Quesadillas:
- Lay out the flour tortillas on a clean work surface.
- Spoon a portion of the chicken and cheese mixture onto one half of each tortilla, spreading it out evenly but leaving a small border around the edges.
- Fold the tortillas over to cover the filling, creating half-moon shapes.

Cook the Quesadillas:
- Heat a large skillet or griddle over medium heat.
- Lightly spray the skillet with cooking spray or brush with a little vegetable oil.
- Place the filled quesadillas onto the skillet and cook for 2-3 minutes on each side, or until they are golden brown and the cheese is melted.
- You may need to cook them in batches depending on the size of your skillet.

Serve:
- Once cooked, transfer the mini chicken quesadillas to a cutting board.
- Use a sharp knife to cut each quesadilla into 2 or 3 wedges, creating mini triangles.
- Arrange the quesadilla wedges on a serving platter.
- Serve warm with your choice of garnishes and dipping sauces, such as salsa, guacamole, sour cream, chopped green onions, or sliced jalapeños.

Tips:

- Customize the filling: Feel free to add other ingredients like diced onions, black beans, corn, or jalapeños to the filling mixture.
- Make ahead: You can assemble the quesadillas ahead of time and cook them just before serving.
- Keep warm: If making a large batch, you can keep the cooked quesadillas warm in a low oven (around 200°F or 95°C) until ready to serve.

These mini chicken quesadillas are perfect for parties, game day snacks, or even a quick and satisfying meal. They are sure to be a crowd-pleaser!

Pesto Tortellini Skewers

Ingredients:

- 1 package (about 9 oz) fresh cheese tortellini
- 1/2 cup store-bought or homemade basil pesto
- Cherry tomatoes
- Fresh mozzarella balls (bocconcini)
- Fresh basil leaves, for garnish
- Wooden skewers or toothpicks

Instructions:

Cook the Tortellini:
- Bring a pot of salted water to a boil. Cook the fresh cheese tortellini according to the package instructions until they are tender. Drain and rinse under cold water to cool them down.

Assemble the Skewers:
- Once the tortellini are cooled, transfer them to a mixing bowl.
- Add the basil pesto to the cooked tortellini and toss to coat them evenly.

Prepare the Ingredients:
- If using wooden skewers, soak them in water for about 10-15 minutes to prevent them from burning.
- Prepare your cherry tomatoes and fresh mozzarella balls. You can leave the mozzarella balls whole or cut them in half, depending on their size.

Assemble the Skewers:
- Thread a cooked tortellini onto a skewer, followed by a cherry tomato, a fresh mozzarella ball (or half), and a fresh basil leaf.
- Repeat the process with the remaining ingredients, alternating the components on each skewer.

Arrange and Garnish:
- Arrange the assembled pesto tortellini skewers on a serving platter.
- Garnish the platter with additional fresh basil leaves for a vibrant and fresh touch.

Serve:
- Serve the pesto tortellini skewers immediately or refrigerate them until ready to serve.
- These skewers can be enjoyed at room temperature or slightly chilled.

Tips:

- Customize the Ingredients: Feel free to add other ingredients such as marinated artichoke hearts, olives, or roasted red peppers to the skewers for additional flavor and variety.
- Make Ahead: You can assemble the skewers a few hours ahead of time and store them in the refrigerator. Just bring them to room temperature before serving.

- Serve with Dipping Sauce: Offer extra pesto or a balsamic glaze on the side for dipping.

These pesto tortellini skewers are not only delicious but also visually appealing. They make a great finger food option for any occasion and are sure to impress your guests! Enjoy making and serving these tasty appetizers.

Coconut Shrimp

Ingredients:

- 1 pound large shrimp, peeled and deveined (tails left on or removed, based on preference)
- 1 cup sweetened shredded coconut
- 1 cup panko breadcrumbs
- 1/2 cup all-purpose flour
- 2 large eggs
- 1/2 teaspoon salt, plus extra for seasoning
- 1/4 teaspoon black pepper
- Vegetable oil, for frying
- Dipping sauce of choice (e.g., sweet chili sauce, mango salsa, or tartar sauce)

Instructions:

Prepare Shrimp:
- Pat the peeled and deveined shrimp dry with paper towels. Season them lightly with salt and pepper.

Set Up Breading Station:
- Prepare three shallow dishes or bowls:
    - Bowl 1: Place all-purpose flour seasoned with 1/2 teaspoon salt.
    - Bowl 2: Whisk eggs until well beaten.
    - Bowl 3: Combine shredded coconut and panko breadcrumbs.

Bread the Shrimp:
- Coat each shrimp in the flour mixture, shaking off any excess.
- Dip the floured shrimp into the beaten eggs, allowing any excess egg to drip off.
- Press the shrimp into the coconut and breadcrumb mixture, ensuring they are well coated. Gently press the coating onto the shrimp to help it adhere.

Fry the Coconut Shrimp:
- In a large skillet or frying pan, heat enough vegetable oil to cover the bottom of the pan over medium-high heat.
- Once the oil is hot (around 350°F or 175°C), carefully add the coated shrimp in batches, making sure not to overcrowd the pan.
- Fry the shrimp for 2-3 minutes on each side, or until they are golden brown and crispy. Use tongs to turn them over halfway through cooking.
- Remove the cooked shrimp from the oil and place them on a plate lined with paper towels to drain any excess oil.

- Repeat the frying process with the remaining shrimp.

Serve:
- Arrange the crispy coconut shrimp on a serving platter.
- Serve them hot with your choice of dipping sauce on the side.

Tips:

- For a lighter option, you can bake the coconut shrimp instead of frying. Preheat your oven to 400°F (200°C) and place the breaded shrimp on a baking sheet lined with parchment paper. Lightly spray the shrimp with cooking spray and bake for about 12-15 minutes, or until golden and crispy.
- Make sure the oil is at the right temperature before frying to achieve crispy shrimp without absorbing too much oil.
- Serve the coconut shrimp as an appetizer with dipping sauce, or as a main dish with a side of rice and vegetables.

Enjoy this crispy and flavorful coconut shrimp recipe for a delicious tropical-inspired dish!

Prosciutto-Wrapped Melon

Ingredients:

- Ripe cantaloupe or honeydew melon
- Thinly sliced prosciutto
- Fresh basil leaves (optional)
- Balsamic glaze (optional, for drizzling)
- Toothpicks or small skewers

Instructions:

Prepare the Melon:
- Choose a ripe cantaloupe or honeydew melon. Slice the melon in half, scoop out the seeds, and remove the rind.
- Cut the melon into bite-sized cubes or wedges. You can also use a melon baller to create small melon balls.

Wrap with Prosciutto:
- Take a slice of prosciutto and cut it lengthwise into thinner strips, if needed.
- Take a strip of prosciutto and wrap it around each piece of melon. You can wrap the prosciutto loosely or stretch it slightly for a snug fit.
- If desired, you can add a small basil leaf between the prosciutto and melon for extra flavor.

Secure with Toothpicks:
- Secure each prosciutto-wrapped melon piece with a toothpick or small skewer to hold everything together.

Arrange and Serve:
- Arrange the prosciutto-wrapped melon pieces on a serving platter.
- Optional: Drizzle a little balsamic glaze over the appetizers for added flavor and presentation.

Serve and Enjoy:
- Serve the prosciutto-wrapped melon as a delightful appetizer or party snack.
- These can be served chilled or at room temperature, depending on your preference.

Tips:

- Choose ripe and sweet melons for the best flavor contrast with the salty prosciutto.
- Feel free to get creative with presentation by arranging the appetizers on a bed of fresh greens or garnishing with additional herbs.
- You can also experiment with different types of melon and cured meats (such as honeydew with speck or other types of ham).

Prosciutto-wrapped melon is a perfect choice for summer gatherings, cocktail parties, or any occasion where you want to impress guests with a simple yet elegant appetizer. Enjoy the delightful combination of flavors and textures in this classic dish!

Crab Cakes

Ingredients:

- 1 pound lump crab meat, drained and picked over for shells
- 1/2 cup breadcrumbs (panko or regular)
- 1/4 cup mayonnaise
- 1 large egg
- 1 tablespoon Dijon mustard
- 1 tablespoon Worcestershire sauce
- 2 green onions, finely chopped
- 1/4 cup finely chopped bell pepper (red or green)
- 2 tablespoons chopped fresh parsley
- 1/2 teaspoon Old Bay seasoning (or seafood seasoning of choice)
- Salt and pepper, to taste
- 1/4 cup vegetable oil or butter, for frying
- Lemon wedges, for serving
- Tartar sauce or remoulade sauce, for serving (optional)

Instructions:

Prepare Crab Cake Mixture:
- In a large bowl, combine the breadcrumbs, mayonnaise, egg, Dijon mustard, Worcestershire sauce, green onions, bell pepper, parsley, Old Bay seasoning, salt, and pepper. Mix well to combine.
- Gently fold in the lump crab meat, being careful not to break up the crab too much. You want the mixture to hold together but still have visible pieces of crab.

Form Crab Cakes:
- Divide the crab mixture into equal portions and shape them into patties, about 1/2 to 3/4 inch thick. Place the formed crab cakes on a baking sheet lined with parchment paper.

Chill Crab Cakes:
- Refrigerate the crab cakes for at least 30 minutes to help them firm up before cooking. This will also enhance the flavors.

Cook Crab Cakes:
- Heat the vegetable oil or melt the butter in a large skillet over medium-high heat.
- Carefully add the crab cakes to the skillet, working in batches if necessary to avoid overcrowding.

- Cook the crab cakes for 3-4 minutes on each side, or until they are golden brown and heated through. Use a spatula to gently flip them over.

Serve Crab Cakes:
- Transfer the cooked crab cakes to a serving platter.
- Serve hot with lemon wedges and your choice of dipping sauce, such as tartar sauce or remoulade sauce.

Tips:

- Use fresh lump crab meat for the best flavor and texture. You can find canned or pasteurized crab meat in the seafood section of most grocery stores.
- Adjust the seasoning to your taste. You can add more Old Bay seasoning or spices like cayenne pepper for extra heat.
- If you prefer a crispy coating, you can dredge the crab cakes in additional breadcrumbs before frying.
- Serve the crab cakes as an appetizer with a salad, or as a main course with sides like coleslaw, rice, or roasted vegetables.

These homemade crab cakes are sure to impress your family and guests with their delicious flavor and crispy texture. Enjoy this classic seafood dish for any occasion!

Mini Reuben Sandwiches

Ingredients:

- Cocktail rye bread slices (or regular rye bread, cut into smaller squares)
- Thinly sliced corned beef
- Swiss cheese slices, cut into smaller pieces to fit the bread
- Sauerkraut, drained and squeezed dry
- Russian dressing (store-bought or homemade)
- Butter or margarine, softened

Instructions:

Assemble the Mini Sandwiches:
- Lay out half of the cocktail rye bread slices on a clean surface.
- Spread a thin layer of Russian dressing on each slice of bread.

Layer the Fillings:
- Top each slice of bread with a piece of Swiss cheese, followed by a small amount of drained sauerkraut, and finally a slice of corned beef.

Top with More Bread:
- Place the remaining slices of cocktail rye bread on top of the corned beef to form mini sandwiches.

Grill the Sandwiches:
- Heat a large skillet or griddle over medium heat.
- Spread a little softened butter or margarine on the outside of each mini sandwich.
- Place the sandwiches in the skillet and cook for 2-3 minutes on each side, or until the bread is golden brown and the cheese is melted.

Serve:
- Remove the grilled mini Reuben sandwiches from the skillet and let them cool slightly.
- Cut each sandwich into quarters or halves, depending on the size of your bread slices.
- Arrange the mini sandwiches on a serving platter and serve warm.

Tips:

- Russian Dressing: If you don't have Russian dressing, you can substitute with Thousand Island dressing.
- Make-Ahead Option: You can assemble the mini sandwiches ahead of time and grill them just before serving to ensure they are warm and crispy.
- Variation: For a vegetarian option, substitute corned beef with sliced mushrooms or tempeh, and use a vegetarian-friendly Russian dressing.

These mini Reuben sandwiches are perfect for parties, game day gatherings, or any occasion where you want to serve a delicious and crowd-pleasing appetizer. Enjoy the classic flavors of a Reuben sandwich in a bite-sized format!

Spanakopita Triangles

Ingredients:

- 1 package (about 10 oz) frozen chopped spinach, thawed and squeezed dry
- 1 cup crumbled feta cheese
- 1/2 cup ricotta cheese or cottage cheese
- 1/4 cup grated Parmesan cheese
- 2 green onions, finely chopped
- 2 tablespoons chopped fresh dill (or 1 tablespoon dried dill)
- 1 tablespoon chopped fresh parsley
- 1/4 teaspoon salt
- 1/4 teaspoon black pepper
- 1/4 teaspoon nutmeg (optional)
- 1/4 cup olive oil, plus more for brushing
- 1 package (about 16 oz) phyllo pastry sheets, thawed if frozen
- Melted butter (optional, for brushing)
- Sesame seeds (optional, for garnish)

Instructions:

Prepare the Filling:
- In a large bowl, combine the chopped spinach, crumbled feta cheese, ricotta or cottage cheese, grated Parmesan cheese, chopped green onions, fresh dill, fresh parsley, salt, black pepper, and nutmeg (if using). Mix well to combine all the ingredients.

Assemble the Spanakopita Triangles:
- Preheat your oven to 375°F (190°C) and line a baking sheet with parchment paper.
- Unroll the phyllo pastry sheets and cover them with a damp towel to prevent them from drying out.
- Take one sheet of phyllo pastry and brush it lightly with olive oil or melted butter. Place another sheet on top and brush with oil again. Repeat with a third sheet.
- Cut the layered phyllo sheets lengthwise into 3 strips (about 3 inches wide).

Fill and Fold the Triangles:
- Place a spoonful of the spinach and cheese filling at the bottom corner of each strip of phyllo.
- Fold one corner of the phyllo diagonally over the filling to form a triangle. Continue folding the triangle sideways (like folding a flag) until you reach the end of the strip. Press the edges to seal.
- Repeat with the remaining phyllo strips and filling mixture.

Bake the Spanakopita Triangles:
- Place the assembled spanakopita triangles on the prepared baking sheet.
- Brush the tops of the triangles with a little more olive oil or melted butter.

- If desired, sprinkle sesame seeds over the tops of the triangles for added crunch and flavor.
- Bake in the preheated oven for 20-25 minutes, or until the triangles are golden brown and crispy.

Serve and Enjoy:
- Remove the spanakopita triangles from the oven and let them cool slightly before serving.
- Serve warm as a delicious appetizer or snack.

Tips:

- Phyllo Pastry Handling: Work quickly with phyllo pastry and keep the sheets covered with a damp towel to prevent them from drying out.
- Make-Ahead Option: You can assemble the spanakopita triangles ahead of time and freeze them before baking. When ready to serve, bake them directly from frozen (adding a few extra minutes of baking time).
- Customize the Filling: Feel free to add chopped onions or garlic to the filling mixture for extra flavor.

These homemade spanakopita triangles are a fantastic addition to any party or gathering. They are crispy, flavorful, and perfect for serving as finger food. Enjoy the taste of Greek cuisine with these delightful appetizers!

Antipasto Skewers

Ingredients:

- Cherry tomatoes
- Fresh mozzarella balls (bocconcini)
- Slices of salami or pepperoni, folded or rolled
- Marinated artichoke hearts, drained and halved
- Pitted black or green olives
- Basil leaves
- Extra virgin olive oil
- Balsamic glaze (optional)
- Wooden skewers or toothpicks

Instructions:

Prepare Ingredients:
- If using wooden skewers, soak them in water for about 10-15 minutes to prevent them from burning.
- Prepare all the ingredients by draining the marinated artichoke hearts and patting them dry with a paper towel. Cut any large ingredients into bite-sized pieces if necessary.

Assemble the Skewers:
- Thread the ingredients onto the skewers in a desired pattern. You can customize the order of ingredients based on your preference.
- Start with a cherry tomato, followed by a folded slice of salami or pepperoni, a mozzarella ball, a basil leaf, a piece of marinated artichoke heart, and finish with an olive.
- Repeat this pattern on each skewer until all ingredients are used.

Drizzle with Olive Oil:
- Arrange the assembled antipasto skewers on a serving platter.
- Drizzle extra virgin olive oil over the skewers to add flavor and shine.

Optional Garnish:
- If desired, drizzle balsamic glaze over the skewers for a touch of sweetness and acidity.

Serve and Enjoy:
- Serve the antipasto skewers as a delightful appetizer or finger food.
- These skewers can be served at room temperature and are perfect for parties, gatherings, or as part of an Italian-themed meal.

Tips:

- Customize Ingredients: Feel free to add or substitute ingredients based on your preference. Other options include marinated cherry peppers, roasted red peppers, prosciutto, or grilled vegetables.

- Make-Ahead Option: You can assemble the antipasto skewers ahead of time and refrigerate them until ready to serve. Just drizzle with olive oil and balsamic glaze right before serving.
- Presentation: Arrange the skewers on a decorative platter and garnish with fresh herbs, such as parsley or oregano, for an attractive presentation.

These antipasto skewers are not only delicious but also visually appealing with a variety of colors and flavors. They are sure to be a hit at any party or gathering! Enjoy creating these tasty Italian-inspired appetizers for your next event.

Buffalo Cauliflower Bites

Ingredients:

- 1 head of cauliflower, cut into florets
- 1 cup all-purpose flour (or chickpea flour for a gluten-free option)
- 1 cup water
- 1 teaspoon garlic powder
- 1 teaspoon onion powder
- 1/2 teaspoon paprika
- Salt and pepper, to taste
- 1 cup buffalo hot sauce (such as Frank's RedHot)
- 1/4 cup unsalted butter, melted (or use vegan butter for a vegan option)
- Optional for serving: Ranch or blue cheese dressing, celery sticks

Instructions:

Preheat the Oven:
- Preheat your oven to 450°F (230°C). Line a baking sheet with parchment paper or lightly grease it with cooking spray.

Prepare the Cauliflower:
- Wash the cauliflower head and cut it into bite-sized florets.
- In a large bowl, whisk together the flour, water, garlic powder, onion powder, paprika, salt, and pepper to create a batter.

Coat the Cauliflower:
- Add the cauliflower florets to the batter and toss until they are evenly coated.

Bake the Cauliflower:
- Spread the coated cauliflower florets in a single layer on the prepared baking sheet.
- Bake in the preheated oven for 20-25 minutes, or until the cauliflower is golden and crispy, flipping halfway through baking for even browning.

Prepare the Buffalo Sauce:
- While the cauliflower is baking, mix together the buffalo hot sauce and melted butter in a bowl.

Toss with Buffalo Sauce:
- Once the cauliflower is done baking, transfer the hot cauliflower florets to a large mixing bowl.
- Pour the buffalo sauce mixture over the cauliflower and toss until the florets are well coated with the sauce.

Serve:
- Transfer the buffalo cauliflower bites to a serving platter.
- Serve hot with ranch or blue cheese dressing for dipping and celery sticks on the side.

Tips:

- Adjust Spiciness: Increase or decrease the amount of buffalo hot sauce based on your spice preference.
- Crispy Texture: For extra crispy cauliflower, you can use a wire rack on top of the baking sheet to allow air circulation around the florets while baking.
- Customize: Feel free to add additional seasonings or spices to the batter for more flavor variation.

These buffalo cauliflower bites are a crowd-pleasing appetizer that's perfect for game day parties, gatherings, or anytime you're craving a spicy and satisfying snack. Enjoy the crispy texture and tangy buffalo sauce flavor without the meat!

Meatball Sliders

Ingredients:

For the Meatballs:

- 1 pound ground beef (or a mix of beef and pork)
- 1/2 cup breadcrumbs
- 1/4 cup grated Parmesan cheese
- 1/4 cup chopped fresh parsley
- 1 egg
- 2 cloves garlic, minced
- 1 teaspoon salt
- 1/2 teaspoon black pepper
- 1/2 teaspoon dried oregano
- 1/4 teaspoon red pepper flakes (optional)
- Olive oil, for cooking

For Assembling the Sliders:

- Slider buns (mini burger buns)
- Marinara sauce, warmed
- Sliced mozzarella or provolone cheese
- Additional grated Parmesan cheese, for topping
- Chopped fresh basil or parsley, for garnish

Instructions:

Make the Meatballs:
- Preheat your oven to 400°F (200°C). Line a baking sheet with parchment paper or lightly grease it with olive oil.
- In a large mixing bowl, combine the ground beef, breadcrumbs, grated Parmesan cheese, chopped parsley, egg, minced garlic, salt, black pepper, oregano, and red pepper flakes (if using). Mix well until all ingredients are evenly incorporated.
- Roll the mixture into small meatballs, about 1 inch in diameter, and place them on the prepared baking sheet.
- Bake the meatballs in the preheated oven for 15-20 minutes, or until they are cooked through and browned on the outside.

Assemble the Sliders:
- Preheat your broiler or oven to melt cheese on the sliders.

- Slice the slider buns in half horizontally and place them on a baking sheet.
- Spread a spoonful of warmed marinara sauce on the bottom half of each slider bun.
- Place a cooked meatball on top of the marinara sauce on each bun.
- Spoon a little more marinara sauce over each meatball.
- Top each meatball with a slice of mozzarella or provolone cheese.
- Place the baking sheet under the broiler or in the oven for 1-2 minutes, or until the cheese is melted and bubbly.
- Remove the sliders from the oven and sprinkle with additional grated Parmesan cheese and chopped fresh basil or parsley.

Serve and Enjoy:
- Place the top half of each slider bun over the cheese-topped meatball.
- Secure each slider with a toothpick if needed.
- Arrange the meatball sliders on a serving platter and serve warm.

Tips:

- Customize the Meatballs: Feel free to use your favorite ground meat mixture for the meatballs, such as ground turkey or chicken.
- Make-Ahead: You can prepare the meatballs in advance and store them in the refrigerator. When ready to serve, assemble the sliders and heat them in the oven until the cheese is melted.
- Side Suggestions: Serve the meatball sliders with additional marinara sauce for dipping or a side salad for a complete meal.

These meatball sliders are sure to be a hit at parties, game day gatherings, or family dinners. Enjoy the savory flavors and cheesy goodness in each bite!

Phyllo-Wrapped Asparagus

Ingredients:

- 1 bunch of asparagus spears, woody ends trimmed
- Olive oil or melted butter, for brushing
- Salt and pepper, to taste
- Phyllo pastry sheets (you will need about 6-8 sheets)
- 1/4 cup grated Parmesan cheese (optional)
- Lemon wedges, for serving

Instructions:

Preheat Oven:
- Preheat your oven to 375°F (190°C). Line a baking sheet with parchment paper or lightly grease it with olive oil.

Prepare Asparagus:
- Wash and trim the asparagus spears to remove the tough woody ends.
- Toss the asparagus spears with a drizzle of olive oil or melted butter, and season with salt and pepper.

Prepare Phyllo Pastry:
- Place one sheet of phyllo pastry on a clean work surface. Brush the sheet lightly with olive oil or melted butter.
- Place another sheet of phyllo pastry on top of the first sheet and brush with oil or butter.
- Repeat with a third sheet of phyllo pastry, brushing with oil or butter.

Cut and Wrap Asparagus:
- Cut the layered phyllo pastry into strips about 3 inches wide.
- Place an asparagus spear at the bottom end of each phyllo strip.
- Roll the asparagus spear up in the phyllo pastry, forming a bundle. Continue wrapping until the entire spear is covered.
- Place the phyllo-wrapped asparagus bundle on the prepared baking sheet.
- Repeat with the remaining asparagus spears and phyllo pastry.

Bake:
- Brush the tops of the phyllo-wrapped asparagus bundles with a little more olive oil or melted butter.
- Sprinkle grated Parmesan cheese over the bundles, if desired, for extra flavor and texture.
- Bake in the preheated oven for 15-20 minutes, or until the phyllo pastry is golden brown and crispy, and the asparagus is tender.

Serve:
- Remove the phyllo-wrapped asparagus bundles from the oven and let them cool slightly.
- Serve the bundles warm with lemon wedges for squeezing over the asparagus.

Tips:

- Handle Phyllo Pastry Carefully: Phyllo pastry can dry out quickly, so keep it covered with a damp towel while working to prevent it from becoming brittle.
- Customize the Filling: You can add a sprinkle of finely chopped herbs or spices to the asparagus before wrapping with phyllo pastry for extra flavor.
- Make-Ahead Option: You can assemble the phyllo-wrapped asparagus bundles ahead of time and refrigerate them until ready to bake. Just brush with oil or butter and bake as directed before serving.

These phyllo-wrapped asparagus bundles make a lovely appetizer or side dish for any occasion. Enjoy the crispy pastry combined with the tender and flavorful asparagus!

Mini Quiche

Ingredients:

- 1 package (14 oz) refrigerated pie crust dough (or homemade pie crust)
- 4 large eggs
- 1/2 cup milk or heavy cream
- Salt and pepper, to taste
- Fillings of your choice (e.g., chopped vegetables, cooked bacon or ham, shredded cheese, spinach, mushrooms, onions, etc.)

Instructions:

Preheat Oven:
- Preheat your oven to 375°F (190°C). Lightly grease a mini muffin tin with cooking spray or butter.

Prepare Pie Crust:
- Roll out the pie crust dough on a lightly floured surface. Use a round cookie cutter or a drinking glass to cut out circles slightly larger than the size of each muffin cup in the tin.
- Press each circle of dough into the muffin cups, forming mini pie crusts.

Prepare Quiche Filling:
- In a mixing bowl, whisk together the eggs, milk or cream, salt, and pepper until well combined.

Assemble Mini Quiches:
- Place a small amount of your chosen fillings into each mini pie crust in the muffin tin. Make sure not to overfill the crusts.
- Pour the egg mixture over the fillings in each mini quiche cup, filling almost to the top but leaving a little space to prevent overflow.

Bake:
- Bake the mini quiches in the preheated oven for 15-20 minutes, or until the egg mixture is set and the crusts are golden brown.

Serve:
- Remove the mini quiches from the oven and let them cool slightly in the muffin tin.
- Carefully remove the mini quiches from the tin and transfer them to a serving platter.
- Serve warm or at room temperature.

Tips:

- Customize Fillings: Feel free to use any combination of fillings you like, such as sautéed vegetables, cooked bacon or ham, shredded cheese, spinach, mushrooms, onions, etc.
- Make-Ahead Option: You can prepare the mini quiches in advance and refrigerate or freeze them before baking. When ready to serve, bake them directly from the refrigerator (adding a few extra minutes of baking time) or thawed if frozen.
- Serving Suggestions: Serve the mini quiches as appetizers, brunch bites, or part of a party spread. They are delicious on their own or with a side salad.

These mini quiches are versatile and can be enjoyed warm or at room temperature. Experiment with different fillings to create a variety of flavors and enjoy these delightful bite-sized treats!

Deviled Eggs

Ingredients:

- 6 large eggs
- 1/4 cup mayonnaise
- 1 teaspoon Dijon mustard
- 1 tablespoon finely chopped fresh chives or green onions
- 1/4 teaspoon garlic powder
- Salt and pepper, to taste
- Paprika or chopped fresh herbs, for garnish

Instructions:

Hard-Boil the Eggs:
- Place the eggs in a saucepan and cover them with water. Bring the water to a boil over high heat.
- Once boiling, cover the saucepan with a lid, remove it from the heat, and let the eggs sit in the hot water for 12 minutes.
- After 12 minutes, transfer the eggs to a bowl of ice water to cool quickly. Let them cool for a few minutes before peeling.

Prepare the Filling:
- Peel the cooled hard-boiled eggs and slice them in half lengthwise. Carefully remove the yolks and place them in a separate bowl.
- Mash the egg yolks with a fork until they are smooth and crumbly.
- Add the mayonnaise, Dijon mustard, chopped chives or green onions, garlic powder, salt, and pepper to the mashed yolks. Mix well until creamy and well combined.

Fill the Egg Whites:
- Spoon or pipe the yolk mixture back into the hollows of the egg whites, dividing it evenly among the egg halves.
- You can use a spoon or a piping bag fitted with a star tip for a decorative presentation.

Garnish and Serve:
- Sprinkle paprika or chopped fresh herbs (such as parsley or dill) over the filled deviled eggs for garnish.
- Arrange the deviled eggs on a serving platter and serve immediately, or refrigerate until ready to serve.

Tips:

- Variations: Feel free to customize the filling with additional ingredients such as relish, pickle juice, hot sauce, crumbled bacon, or grated cheese.
- Make-Ahead: You can prepare the deviled eggs in advance and store them covered in the refrigerator until ready to serve.

- Serving Suggestions: Deviled eggs are perfect for parties, picnics, potlucks, or as a snack or appetizer. They pair well with a variety of dishes and are always a crowd-pleaser.

Enjoy these classic deviled eggs as a tasty and satisfying appetizer that's easy to make and even easier to enjoy!

Teriyaki Beef Skewers

Ingredients:

- 1 pound beef steak (such as sirloin, flank, or skirt steak), thinly sliced
- 1/4 cup soy sauce (use low-sodium soy sauce if preferred)
- 2 tablespoons honey or brown sugar
- 2 tablespoons mirin (Japanese sweet rice wine) or rice vinegar
- 2 tablespoons sake or dry white wine
- 2 cloves garlic, minced
- 1 teaspoon grated fresh ginger
- 1 tablespoon sesame oil (optional)
- Wooden skewers, soaked in water for 30 minutes to prevent burning
- Sesame seeds and sliced green onions, for garnish (optional)

Instructions:

Prepare the Marinade:
- In a bowl, whisk together the soy sauce, honey or brown sugar, mirin, sake or white wine, minced garlic, grated ginger, and sesame oil (if using) to make the teriyaki marinade.

Marinate the Beef:
- Place the thinly sliced beef in a shallow dish or resealable plastic bag.
- Pour the teriyaki marinade over the beef, ensuring that all pieces are coated. Marinate the beef in the refrigerator for at least 1 hour, or preferably overnight for maximum flavor.

Assemble the Skewers:
- Preheat your grill or broiler.
- Thread the marinated beef slices onto the soaked wooden skewers, folding the slices if necessary to create a layered effect.

Grill or Broil the Skewers:
- Grill the beef skewers over medium-high heat for 2-3 minutes per side, or until the beef is cooked to your desired level of doneness.
- Alternatively, you can broil the skewers in the oven on a foil-lined baking sheet, turning halfway through cooking.

Serve:
- Transfer the cooked teriyaki beef skewers to a serving platter.
- Garnish with sesame seeds and sliced green onions, if desired.
- Serve the skewers hot as an appetizer or main dish, accompanied by rice or noodles.

Tips:

- Beef Selection: Choose a tender cut of beef for best results, such as sirloin, flank, or skirt steak. Slice the beef thinly against the grain for tenderness.
- Customize the Marinade: Feel free to adjust the sweetness or saltiness of the marinade by adding more or less honey or soy sauce, according to your taste preference.
- Serving Suggestions: Serve the teriyaki beef skewers with steamed rice, stir-fried vegetables, or a side salad for a complete meal.
- Alternative Cooking Methods: If you don't have a grill or broiler, you can also cook the beef skewers in a skillet on the stovetop over medium-high heat.

Enjoy these delicious teriyaki beef skewers as a flavorful and satisfying dish that's perfect for any occasion!

Cucumber Smoked Salmon Rolls

Ingredients:

- 1 English cucumber
- 4 ounces (about 113 grams) smoked salmon, thinly sliced
- 4 ounces (about 113 grams) cream cheese or goat cheese, softened
- 1 tablespoon fresh dill, chopped
- 1 tablespoon capers (optional)
- Lemon zest (from 1 lemon)
- Salt and pepper, to taste

Instructions:

Prepare the Cucumber:
- Wash and dry the cucumber. Using a vegetable peeler, slice the cucumber lengthwise into thin, long strips (about 1/16 inch thick). Discard the first strip (mostly skin) and continue peeling until you reach the seedy core. You should get about 12-16 strips.

Prepare the Filling:
- In a bowl, mix together the softened cream cheese or goat cheese with chopped fresh dill, capers (if using), lemon zest, salt, and pepper. Adjust seasoning to taste.

Assemble the Rolls:
- Lay out the cucumber strips on a clean work surface.
- Spread a thin layer of the cheese mixture onto each cucumber strip, covering the entire surface.
- Place a slice of smoked salmon on top of the cheese mixture, covering about half of the cucumber strip.

Roll Up the Rolls:
- Starting from one end, tightly roll up each cucumber strip with the salmon and cheese filling inside.
- Secure the end of each roll with a toothpick to hold it together.

Chill and Serve:
- Place the cucumber smoked salmon rolls on a serving platter.
- Cover and refrigerate the rolls for at least 30 minutes to allow them to set and chill.
- Before serving, garnish with additional fresh dill and lemon zest if desired.

Serve and Enjoy:
- Arrange the chilled cucumber smoked salmon rolls on a serving platter.
- Serve as an elegant appetizer or light snack for parties or gatherings.

Tips:

- Customize the Filling: Feel free to add chopped chives, minced shallots, or a splash of lemon juice to the cheese mixture for extra flavor.
- Make-Ahead Option: You can assemble the cucumber smoked salmon rolls a few hours in advance and refrigerate them until ready to serve.
- Serving Suggestions: Serve the rolls on their own as appetizers or alongside a salad for a light and refreshing meal.

These cucumber smoked salmon rolls are not only delicious but also visually appealing with their vibrant colors and flavors. Enjoy the combination of cool cucumber, creamy cheese, and smoky salmon in every bite!

Chicken Satay Skewers

Ingredients:

For the Chicken Satay:

- 1 pound boneless, skinless chicken breasts or thighs, cut into thin strips
- Wooden skewers, soaked in water for 30 minutes
- 2 tablespoons soy sauce
- 2 tablespoons fish sauce
- 2 tablespoons brown sugar
- 2 tablespoons vegetable oil
- 2 cloves garlic, minced
- 1 teaspoon ground coriander
- 1 teaspoon ground cumin
- 1/2 teaspoon turmeric
- 1/4 teaspoon cayenne pepper (adjust to taste)
- Lime wedges, for serving
- Chopped fresh cilantro or green onions, for garnish

For the Peanut Sauce:

- 1/2 cup creamy peanut butter
- 1/4 cup coconut milk
- 2 tablespoons soy sauce
- 1 tablespoon brown sugar
- 1 tablespoon lime juice
- 1 teaspoon grated ginger
- 1 clove garlic, minced
- Water (as needed to adjust consistency)

Instructions:

Prepare the Chicken Marinade:
- In a bowl, whisk together soy sauce, fish sauce, brown sugar, vegetable oil, minced garlic, ground coriander, ground cumin, turmeric, and cayenne pepper.

Marinate the Chicken:
- Place the chicken strips in a shallow dish or resealable plastic bag.
- Pour the marinade over the chicken, making sure all pieces are coated. Cover and refrigerate for at least 1 hour, or preferably overnight for best flavor.

Make the Peanut Sauce:
- In a saucepan over medium heat, combine peanut butter, coconut milk, soy sauce, brown sugar, lime juice, grated ginger, and minced garlic.

- Stir until smooth and well combined. If the sauce is too thick, add water gradually to reach desired consistency. Simmer gently for a few minutes, then remove from heat.

Skewer and Grill the Chicken:
- Preheat your grill or grill pan over medium-high heat.
- Thread the marinated chicken strips onto the soaked wooden skewers.
- Grill the chicken skewers for 3-4 minutes on each side, or until cooked through and nicely charred.

Serve:
- Arrange the grilled chicken satay skewers on a serving platter.
- Drizzle with some of the peanut sauce or serve the sauce on the side for dipping.
- Garnish with lime wedges and chopped fresh cilantro or green onions.

Enjoy:
- Serve the chicken satay skewers hot as an appetizer or main dish.
- Enjoy with steamed rice, cucumber salad, or other side dishes of your choice.

Tips:

- Alternative Cooking Methods: If you don't have a grill, you can cook the chicken skewers in a broiler or on a stovetop grill pan.
- Customize: Feel free to adjust the level of spiciness in the marinade by adding more or less cayenne pepper.
- Make-Ahead: You can prepare the marinade and peanut sauce in advance and store them in the refrigerator until ready to use.

These chicken satay skewers with peanut sauce are bursting with flavor and make a fantastic appetizer or main course. Enjoy the delicious combination of tender chicken and savory-sweet peanut sauce!

Stuffed Cherry Tomatoes

Ingredients:

- 24-30 cherry tomatoes
- 4 ounces cream cheese, softened
- 2 tablespoons mayonnaise
- 2 tablespoons finely chopped fresh herbs (such as basil, chives, or parsley)
- 1 tablespoon finely chopped green onions or chives
- Salt and pepper, to taste
- Optional garnish: Fresh herb leaves (basil, parsley) or additional chopped chives

Instructions:

Prepare the Cherry Tomatoes:
- Wash the cherry tomatoes and pat them dry with a paper towel.
- Slice off the top (stem end) of each cherry tomato and use a small spoon or melon baller to scoop out the seeds and pulp, creating a small cavity. Be careful not to cut through the bottom of the tomatoes.

Make the Filling:
- In a mixing bowl, combine the softened cream cheese, mayonnaise, finely chopped herbs, and green onions or chives.
- Season the mixture with salt and pepper to taste. Stir until well combined and smooth.

Fill the Cherry Tomatoes:
- Use a small spoon or a piping bag fitted with a star tip to fill each cherry tomato cavity with the cream cheese mixture.
- Fill the tomatoes until the filling is slightly mounded on top.

Garnish and Serve:
- Arrange the stuffed cherry tomatoes on a serving platter.
- Garnish the top of each tomato with a small herb leaf (such as basil or parsley) or sprinkle with additional chopped chives for decoration.

Chill and Serve:
- Refrigerate the stuffed cherry tomatoes for at least 30 minutes to allow the filling to set and the flavors to meld.

Enjoy:
- Serve the stuffed cherry tomatoes chilled as an appetizer or part of a party spread.
- Enjoy these bite-sized treats with a glass of wine or alongside other appetizers.

Tips:

- Variety of Fillings: Feel free to customize the filling by adding minced garlic, grated Parmesan cheese, crumbled bacon, or finely chopped olives for extra flavor.

- Make-Ahead: You can prepare the cream cheese filling and scoop out the cherry tomatoes in advance. Store the filling and hollowed-out tomatoes separately in the refrigerator, then assemble and chill before serving.
- Serving Suggestions: Serve the stuffed cherry tomatoes on a decorative platter with toothpicks or small skewers for easy serving.

These stuffed cherry tomatoes are not only delicious but also visually appealing, making them a perfect addition to any party or gathering. Enjoy the creamy filling and burst of flavor in each bite!

Jalapeño Poppers

Ingredients:

- 12 fresh jalapeño peppers
- 8 ounces cream cheese, softened
- 1 cup shredded cheddar cheese (or cheese of your choice)
- 1 teaspoon garlic powder
- 1/2 teaspoon onion powder
- Salt and pepper, to taste
- 1 cup breadcrumbs (plain or seasoned)
- 2 large eggs, beaten
- Cooking oil (if frying)
- Optional: Ranch dressing or sour cream, for dipping

Instructions:

Prepare the Jalapeño Peppers:
- Wash the jalapeño peppers and cut them in half lengthwise. Use a spoon to remove the seeds and membranes, creating hollow jalapeño halves. Wear gloves to protect your hands from the heat of the peppers.

Make the Filling:
- In a mixing bowl, combine the softened cream cheese, shredded cheddar cheese, garlic powder, onion powder, salt, and pepper. Mix until smooth and well combined.

Fill the Jalapeño Halves:
- Use a spoon or piping bag to fill each jalapeño half with the cream cheese mixture, pressing it in slightly to ensure each pepper is fully filled.

Bread the Jalapeño Poppers:
- Prepare two shallow bowls: one with beaten eggs and another with breadcrumbs.
- Dip each filled jalapeño half into the beaten eggs, coating it completely.
- Next, roll the jalapeño in the breadcrumbs, pressing gently to adhere the breadcrumbs to the cream cheese filling.
- Place the breaded jalapeño poppers on a baking sheet lined with parchment paper.

Bake or Fry the Jalapeño Poppers:
- Baking Method: Preheat your oven to 375°F (190°C). Arrange the breaded jalapeño poppers on the baking sheet. Bake for 15-20 minutes, or until the jalapeños are tender and the breadcrumbs are golden brown.
- Frying Method: Heat oil in a deep skillet or fryer to 350°F (175°C). Carefully add the breaded jalapeño poppers in batches and fry until golden brown and crispy, about 2-3 minutes per side. Drain on paper towels.

Serve:
- Once cooked, transfer the jalapeño poppers to a serving platter.
- Serve hot with ranch dressing or sour cream on the side for dipping.

Tips:

- Adjusting Heat Level: For milder jalapeño poppers, you can remove all the seeds and membranes. For spicier poppers, leave some or all of the membranes intact.
- Variations: Add cooked and crumbled bacon, chopped green onions, or diced jalapeños to the cream cheese filling for extra flavor.
- Make-Ahead: You can prepare the jalapeño poppers in advance and refrigerate them before baking or frying. Just bake or fry them when ready to serve.

Enjoy these homemade jalapeño poppers as a delicious and crowd-pleasing appetizer for parties, game day, or any occasion. The creamy, cheesy filling pairs perfectly with the crispy exterior of these spicy treats!

Greek Yogurt Dip with Veggie Sticks

Ingredients:

- 1 cup Greek yogurt (plain or flavored)
- 1 tablespoon olive oil
- 1 clove garlic, minced
- 1 tablespoon fresh lemon juice
- 1 tablespoon chopped fresh dill or parsley
- Salt and pepper, to taste
- Assorted fresh vegetables for dipping (carrot sticks, cucumber slices, bell pepper strips, cherry tomatoes, celery sticks, etc.)

Instructions:

Prepare the Greek Yogurt Dip:
- In a mixing bowl, combine the Greek yogurt, olive oil, minced garlic, fresh lemon juice, chopped dill or parsley, salt, and pepper.
- Stir well until all ingredients are thoroughly combined.

Chill the Dip:
- Cover the bowl with plastic wrap and refrigerate the dip for at least 30 minutes to allow the flavors to meld and the dip to slightly thicken.

Prepare the Vegetable Sticks:
- Wash and cut a variety of fresh vegetables into sticks or slices suitable for dipping. Common choices include carrot sticks, cucumber slices, bell pepper strips, cherry tomatoes, and celery sticks.

Serve:
- Transfer the chilled Greek yogurt dip to a serving bowl or platter.
- Arrange the assorted vegetable sticks around the dip for dipping.

Enjoy:
- Serve the Greek yogurt dip with the vegetable sticks as a healthy snack or appetizer.
- Enjoy the creamy dip with the crunchy freshness of the vegetables.

Tips:

- Flavor Variations: Feel free to customize the dip by adding additional herbs or spices such as chopped mint, basil, dill, or a sprinkle of paprika or cayenne pepper for a spicy kick.
- Make-Ahead: You can prepare the Greek yogurt dip in advance and store it in the refrigerator until ready to serve. Give it a stir before serving.
- Serving Suggestions: This dip also pairs well with pita bread or whole-grain crackers in addition to vegetable sticks.

This Greek yogurt dip with veggie sticks is not only delicious and satisfying but also packed with nutrients. It's perfect for parties, gatherings, or a healthy snack any time of the day. Enjoy dipping and savoring the flavors of this nutritious treat!

Crab Stuffed Mushrooms

Ingredients:

- 1 cup Greek yogurt (plain or flavored)
- 1 tablespoon olive oil
- 1 clove garlic, minced
- 1 tablespoon fresh lemon juice
- 1 tablespoon chopped fresh dill or parsley
- Salt and pepper, to taste
- Assorted fresh vegetables for dipping (carrot sticks, cucumber slices, bell pepper strips, cherry tomatoes, celery sticks, etc.)

Instructions:

Prepare the Greek Yogurt Dip:
- In a mixing bowl, combine the Greek yogurt, olive oil, minced garlic, fresh lemon juice, chopped dill or parsley, salt, and pepper.
- Stir well until all ingredients are thoroughly combined.

Chill the Dip:
- Cover the bowl with plastic wrap and refrigerate the dip for at least 30 minutes to allow the flavors to meld and the dip to slightly thicken.

Prepare the Vegetable Sticks:
- Wash and cut a variety of fresh vegetables into sticks or slices suitable for dipping. Common choices include carrot sticks, cucumber slices, bell pepper strips, cherry tomatoes, and celery sticks.

Serve:
- Transfer the chilled Greek yogurt dip to a serving bowl or platter.
- Arrange the assorted vegetable sticks around the dip for dipping.

Enjoy:
- Serve the Greek yogurt dip with the vegetable sticks as a healthy snack or appetizer.
- Enjoy the creamy dip with the crunchy freshness of the vegetables.

Tips:

- Flavor Variations: Feel free to customize the dip by adding additional herbs or spices such as chopped mint, basil, dill, or a sprinkle of paprika or cayenne pepper for a spicy kick.

- Make-Ahead: You can prepare the Greek yogurt dip in advance and store it in the refrigerator until ready to serve. Give it a stir before serving.
- Serving Suggestions: This dip also pairs well with pita bread or whole-grain crackers in addition to vegetable sticks.

This Greek yogurt dip with veggie sticks is not only delicious and satisfying but also packed with nutrients. It's perfect for parties, gatherings, or a healthy snack any time of the day. Enjoy dipping and savoring the flavors of this nutritious treat!

Thai Lettuce Wraps

Caprese Salad Bites

Ingredients:

- Cherry or grape tomatoes
- Fresh mozzarella cheese, cut into small cubes or balls
- Fresh basil leaves
- Balsamic glaze (store-bought or homemade)
- Toothpicks or small skewers

Instructions:

Prepare Ingredients:
- Wash the cherry or grape tomatoes and pat them dry with paper towels.
- Cut the fresh mozzarella cheese into small cubes or use mini mozzarella balls (also known as bocconcini).
- Wash and dry the fresh basil leaves.

Assemble the Caprese Salad Bites:
- Take a toothpick or small skewer and thread on a cherry tomato.
- Follow with a piece of mozzarella cheese.
- Add a fresh basil leaf folded or rolled up.
- Continue assembling more Caprese salad bites until you've used all the ingredients.

Arrange on Serving Platter:
- Arrange the assembled Caprese salad bites on a serving platter or plate. Arrange them neatly in rows or in a circular pattern.

Drizzle with Balsamic Glaze:
- Just before serving, drizzle balsamic glaze over the Caprese salad bites. You can use store-bought balsamic glaze or make your own by reducing balsamic vinegar until it thickens into a syrupy consistency.

Serve and Enjoy:
- Serve the Caprese salad bites immediately. They are best enjoyed fresh and at room temperature.

Tips:

- Use ripe and flavorful cherry or grape tomatoes for the best taste.
- If using larger mozzarella balls, you can cut them into smaller pieces to match the size of the tomatoes.

- For added flavor, sprinkle a little salt and pepper over the assembled Caprese salad bites before drizzling with balsamic glaze.
- Customize the presentation by arranging the bites on decorative toothpicks or skewers with colorful garnishes like fresh herbs or edible flowers.

These Caprese salad bites are a perfect appetizer for any occasion. They are not only delicious but also visually appealing with their vibrant colors and fresh flavors. Enjoy these tasty bites as a delightful starter or party snack!

Mini Beef Wellingtons

Ingredients:

- Beef Fillet (tenderloin), about 1 pound
- Salt and Pepper, to taste
- Olive Oil, for searing
- Dijon Mustard, for brushing
- Puff Pastry, thawed if frozen
- Mushroom Duxelles (finely chopped mushrooms cooked with shallots, garlic, and herbs)
- Egg, beaten (for egg wash)

Instructions:

Prepare the Beef:
- Season the beef fillet generously with salt and pepper.
- In a hot skillet, add a bit of olive oil and sear the beef on all sides until browned (about 1-2 minutes per side). The goal is just to brown the outside, not to cook the meat through. Set aside to cool.

Prepare the Mushroom Duxelles:
- Make a mushroom duxelles by finely chopping mushrooms and cooking them with minced shallots, garlic, and herbs (like thyme or rosemary) until the mixture is dry. Season with salt and pepper. Allow to cool.

Assembly:
- Roll out the puff pastry on a lightly floured surface to a thickness of about 1/4 inch.
- Spread a thin layer of Dijon mustard over the puff pastry.
- Spread a layer of mushroom duxelles over the mustard.

Wrap the Beef:
- Place the seared beef fillet in the center of the pastry.
- Carefully wrap the pastry around the beef, sealing the edges well. Trim any excess pastry if necessary.
- Brush the outside of the pastry with beaten egg to create a golden finish.

Chilling:
- Place the wrapped beef in the refrigerator for at least 15-20 minutes to allow the pastry to firm up.

Baking:
- Preheat your oven to 425°F (220°C).
- Place the wrapped beef on a baking sheet lined with parchment paper.
- Brush the pastry again with the beaten egg.
- Bake for about 20-25 minutes or until the pastry is golden brown and the beef reaches your desired level of doneness (medium-rare is recommended).

Rest and Serve:
- Remove from the oven and let the Mini Beef Wellingtons rest for a few minutes before slicing.

- Serve warm as an appetizer or main course.

Serving Suggestions:

- Mini Beef Wellingtons pair well with a simple green salad dressed with a vinaigrette.
- They can also be served with a creamy sauce like a red wine reduction or a horseradish cream.

Enjoy making these Mini Beef Wellingtons for your next gathering or special occasion! They're sure to impress your guests with their beautiful presentation and delicious flavors.

BBQ Chicken Sliders

Ingredients:

- Chicken Breast or Thighs, boneless and skinless, about 1 pound
- Salt and Pepper, to taste
- Garlic Powder, to taste
- Onion Powder, to taste
- Paprika, to taste
- Olive Oil, for cooking
- BBQ Sauce, your favorite kind
- Slider Buns, small and soft
- Sliced Cheese (optional)
- Sliced Red Onion (optional)
- Lettuce or Coleslaw (optional)

Instructions:

Prepare the Chicken:
- Season the chicken with salt, pepper, garlic powder, onion powder, and paprika. Ensure both sides are evenly seasoned.

Cook the Chicken:
- Heat olive oil in a skillet over medium-high heat.
- Add the seasoned chicken to the skillet and cook for about 5-6 minutes on each side, or until the chicken is fully cooked and no longer pink inside.
- Once cooked, remove the chicken from the skillet and let it rest for a few minutes before shredding.

Shred the Chicken:
- Using two forks, shred the cooked chicken into bite-sized pieces.

Combine with BBQ Sauce:
- In a mixing bowl, toss the shredded chicken with your favorite BBQ sauce until the chicken is well coated. Adjust the amount of BBQ sauce based on your preference for sauciness.

Assemble the Sliders:
- Split the slider buns in half horizontally.
- Place a portion of the BBQ chicken onto the bottom half of each slider bun.
- Optionally, add a slice of cheese on top of the chicken while it's still warm to allow it to melt slightly.
- Top with sliced red onion, lettuce, or coleslaw for added freshness and crunch.
- Place the top half of the slider bun over the filling.

Serve and Enjoy:
- Arrange the BBQ Chicken Sliders on a serving platter.
- Serve immediately while warm.

Serving Suggestions:

- Offer additional BBQ sauce on the side for dipping.
- Serve with pickles or potato chips on the side for a complete meal.
- These sliders pair well with coleslaw or a simple green salad.

BBQ Chicken Sliders are versatile and can be customized to suit your taste preferences. Feel free to adjust the seasonings, toppings, or type of BBQ sauce used to create your perfect sliders. They're sure to be a hit at your next gathering!

Sweet Potato Rounds with Goat Cheese

Ingredients:

- Sweet Potatoes, 2 large
- Olive Oil, for drizzling
- Salt and Pepper, to taste
- Goat Cheese, crumbled
- Honey, for drizzling (optional)
- Fresh Thyme, chopped (optional, for garnish)

Instructions:

Preheat the Oven:
- Preheat your oven to 400°F (200°C) and line a baking sheet with parchment paper.

Prepare the Sweet Potatoes:
- Wash the sweet potatoes thoroughly and slice them into rounds, about 1/4 to 1/2 inch thick.

Season and Roast:
- Arrange the sweet potato rounds on the prepared baking sheet.
- Drizzle olive oil over the sweet potatoes and season with salt and pepper.

Roast in the Oven:
- Place the baking sheet in the preheated oven and roast the sweet potato rounds for about 20-25 minutes, or until they are tender and lightly golden, flipping them halfway through cooking for even browning.

Assemble the Rounds:
- Once the sweet potato rounds are cooked, remove them from the oven.
- Top each round with crumbled goat cheese while they are still warm. The residual heat will slightly soften the cheese.

Serve:
- Arrange the sweet potato rounds with goat cheese on a serving platter.
- Drizzle honey over the rounds for a touch of sweetness, if desired.
- Garnish with chopped fresh thyme for added flavor and presentation.

Enjoy:
- Serve the sweet potato rounds with goat cheese immediately while warm.

Serving Suggestions:

- Serve these sweet potato rounds as an appetizer for a party or gathering.
- They also make a delicious side dish alongside roasted meats or poultry.
- Experiment with additional toppings such as chopped nuts (like pecans or walnuts) or a balsamic reduction for extra flavor.

These Sweet Potato Rounds with Goat Cheese are sure to impress with their combination of sweet, savory, and creamy flavors. They're a perfect blend of simplicity and elegance that will be enjoyed by all!

Buffalo Chicken Dip Cups

Ingredients:

- Cooked Chicken, shredded or diced (about 2 cups)
- Cream Cheese, softened (8 oz)
- Buffalo Sauce, such as Frank's RedHot (1/2 cup)
- Ranch Dressing, 2-3 tablespoons
- Shredded Mozzarella Cheese, 1 cup
- Wonton Wrappers, 24 (usually found in the refrigerated section)
- Green Onions, thinly sliced (for garnish, optional)
- Cooking Spray

Instructions:

Preheat the Oven:
- Preheat your oven to 375°F (190°C).

Prepare the Filling:
- In a mixing bowl, combine the cooked chicken, softened cream cheese, buffalo sauce, ranch dressing, and shredded mozzarella cheese. Mix until well combined.

Assemble the Dip Cups:
- Lightly grease a mini muffin tin with cooking spray.
- Press a wonton wrapper into each muffin cup, allowing the edges to extend over the top.

Fill the Cups:
- Spoon the buffalo chicken dip mixture into each wonton cup, filling them almost to the top.

Bake:
- Bake in the preheated oven for about 10-12 minutes, or until the wonton wrappers are golden brown and the filling is hot and bubbly.

Garnish and Serve:
- Remove the Buffalo Chicken Dip Cups from the oven and let them cool for a few minutes.
- Carefully remove the cups from the muffin tin and arrange them on a serving platter.
- Garnish with thinly sliced green onions, if desired.

Enjoy:
- Serve the Buffalo Chicken Dip Cups warm, and watch them disappear!

Serving Suggestions:

- Serve these Buffalo Chicken Dip Cups with additional ranch dressing or blue cheese dressing for dipping.
- They pair well with celery sticks or carrot sticks for a crunchy contrast.
- Make sure to have plenty on hand, as these tasty appetizers tend to be a hit at parties!

These Buffalo Chicken Dip Cups are easy to make and perfect for feeding a crowd. They're a fun twist on traditional buffalo chicken dip, with the added convenience of individual servings. Enjoy making and sharing these delicious appetizers!

Mini Tacos

Ingredients:

- Mini Taco Shells (store-bought or homemade)
- Ground Beef or Chicken, cooked and seasoned with taco seasoning
- Refried Beans (optional)
- Shredded Lettuce
- Diced Tomatoes
- Shredded Cheese (such as cheddar or Mexican blend)
- Sour Cream
- Salsa
- Guacamole (optional)
- Chopped Cilantro (for garnish)
- Lime Wedges (for serving)
- Additional toppings of your choice (such as sliced jalapeños, diced onions, or black olives)

Instructions:

Prepare the Taco Filling:
- Cook and season the ground beef or chicken with taco seasoning according to package instructions. Ensure the meat is fully cooked and well-seasoned.

Assemble the Mini Tacos:
- If using store-bought mini taco shells, follow the package instructions for crisping them up before filling.
- Spoon a small amount of refried beans (if using) into each mini taco shell.
- Fill each taco shell with a spoonful of the cooked taco meat.

Add Toppings:
- Top the mini tacos with shredded lettuce, diced tomatoes, shredded cheese, sour cream, salsa, guacamole, and any other toppings you desire.

Garnish and Serve:
- Garnish the mini tacos with chopped cilantro.
- Arrange the mini tacos on a serving platter.
- Serve with lime wedges on the side for squeezing over the tacos.

Tips for Customization:

- Vegetarian Option: Substitute the meat with seasoned black beans or grilled vegetables.
- Seafood Option: Use seasoned shrimp or fish for a seafood twist.
- Spicy Kick: Add sliced jalapeños or a drizzle of hot sauce for extra heat.
- Low-Carb Version: Skip the taco shells and serve the toppings in lettuce cups or on cucumber slices.

Serving Suggestions:

- Mini tacos are perfect for parties, game days, or any gathering where finger foods are served.
- Arrange the mini tacos on a platter with small bowls of toppings for guests to customize their tacos.
- Serve alongside Mexican rice, chips, and salsa for a complete party spread.

These mini tacos are sure to be a hit with friends and family. Feel free to get creative with the toppings and fillings to suit your taste preferences. Enjoy making and serving these delicious mini treats!

Ratatouille Tartlets

Ingredients:

For the Tartlet Shells:

- 1 package (about 14 oz) of store-bought puff pastry, thawed
- All-purpose flour, for dusting

For the Ratatouille Filling:

- 1 small eggplant, diced into small cubes
- 1 zucchini, diced into small cubes
- 1 red bell pepper, diced
- 1 yellow bell pepper, diced
- 1 onion, finely chopped
- 2-3 cloves of garlic, minced
- 2 tablespoons olive oil
- 1 can (14 oz) diced tomatoes
- 1 teaspoon dried thyme
- 1 teaspoon dried oregano
- Salt and pepper, to taste
- Fresh basil leaves, chopped, for garnish
- Grated Parmesan cheese, for garnish (optional)

Instructions:

Prepare the Ratatouille Filling:
- In a large skillet or frying pan, heat olive oil over medium heat.
- Add the chopped onion and garlic, and sauté until softened and fragrant, about 2-3 minutes.
- Add the diced eggplant, zucchini, and bell peppers to the pan. Cook, stirring occasionally, until the vegetables start to soften, about 8-10 minutes.

Add Tomatoes and Seasonings:
- Stir in the diced tomatoes (with their juices), dried thyme, dried oregano, salt, and pepper.
- Continue to cook the mixture over medium heat, stirring occasionally, until the vegetables are tender and the flavors have melded together, about 10-12 minutes.
- Taste and adjust seasoning as needed. Remove from heat and let the ratatouille filling cool slightly.

Prepare the Tartlet Shells:
- Preheat your oven to 400°F (200°C).

- On a lightly floured surface, roll out the thawed puff pastry to about 1/4-inch thickness.
- Using a round cookie cutter or a glass, cut out circles of puff pastry dough slightly larger than the wells of a mini muffin tin.
- Gently press each circle of dough into the wells of the mini muffin tin, forming small tartlet shells.

Assemble and Bake:
- Spoon the cooled ratatouille filling into each tartlet shell, filling them to the top.
- Place the mini muffin tin in the preheated oven and bake for 15-18 minutes, or until the tartlet shells are golden brown and crisp.

Serve:
- Remove the ratatouille tartlets from the oven and let them cool in the muffin tin for a few minutes.
- Carefully remove the tartlets from the tin and transfer them to a serving platter.
- Garnish with chopped fresh basil and grated Parmesan cheese, if desired.
- Serve warm or at room temperature as a delightful appetizer or party snack.

Serving Suggestions:

- Ratatouille tartlets can be served as part of a party spread or as a starter before a meal.
- They pair well with a crisp white wine or a light rosé.
- Enjoy these tartlets alongside a fresh green salad for a complete and satisfying dish.

These ratatouille tartlets are a wonderful way to showcase the flavors of seasonal vegetables in a bite-sized format. They are perfect for entertaining and will surely impress your guests with their taste and presentation. Enjoy making and serving these delicious tartlets!

Coconut Chicken Tenders

Ingredients:

- Chicken Breast, boneless and skinless, cut into strips or tenders
- Salt and Pepper, to taste
- All-purpose Flour, for dredging
- Eggs, beaten (about 2 eggs)
- Shredded Coconut, sweetened or unsweetened (about 1 cup)
- Breadcrumbs, about 1 cup (panko breadcrumbs work well for extra crispiness)
- Vegetable Oil, for frying
- Dipping Sauce (optional), such as sweet chili sauce, honey mustard, or ranch dressing

Instructions:

Prepare the Chicken:
- Season the chicken strips with salt and pepper.

Set Up a Dredging Station:
- Prepare three shallow bowls: one with flour, one with beaten eggs, and one with a mixture of shredded coconut and breadcrumbs (combine the shredded coconut and breadcrumbs together).

Dredge the Chicken Strips:
- Dredge each chicken strip in the flour, shaking off any excess.
- Dip the floured chicken strip into the beaten eggs, allowing any excess to drip off.
- Finally, coat the chicken strip thoroughly with the coconut and breadcrumb mixture, pressing gently to adhere.

Heat the Oil:
- In a large skillet or frying pan, heat enough vegetable oil over medium-high heat to cover the bottom of the pan.

Fry the Chicken Tenders:
- Carefully place the coated chicken tenders into the hot oil, in batches if necessary to avoid overcrowding.
- Fry the chicken tenders for about 3-4 minutes per side, or until they are golden brown and cooked through. Use tongs to flip them halfway through cooking.
- Adjust the heat as needed to maintain a steady temperature and prevent burning.

Drain and Serve:
- Once cooked, transfer the coconut chicken tenders to a plate lined with paper towels to drain excess oil.

Serve with Dipping Sauce:
- Serve the coconut chicken tenders warm with your favorite dipping sauce on the side.

Tips for Success:

- Make sure the oil is hot enough before adding the chicken tenders to ensure they become crispy and golden brown.
- For extra coconut flavor, you can add a bit of coconut milk to the beaten eggs.
- If you prefer baking instead of frying, you can arrange the breaded chicken tenders on a baking sheet lined with parchment paper and bake in a preheated oven at 400°F (200°C) for about 20-25 minutes, turning halfway through, until golden and cooked through.

Coconut chicken tenders are sure to be a hit with family and friends. They are crunchy on the outside, juicy on the inside, and packed with tropical coconut flavor. Enjoy these delicious tenders as a snack, appetizer, or main course served with a side salad or rice.

Tomato Basil Bruschetta

Ingredients:

- Ripe Tomatoes, about 4 medium-sized, diced
- Fresh Basil Leaves, chopped (about 1/2 cup)
- Garlic Cloves, minced (2-3 cloves)
- Extra Virgin Olive Oil, 1/4 cup
- Balsamic Vinegar, 1 tablespoon (optional)
- Salt and Pepper, to taste
- Baguette or Italian Bread, sliced into 1/2-inch thick pieces
- Olive Oil, for brushing bread
- Garlic Clove, for rubbing on bread (optional)

Instructions:

Prepare the Tomato Basil Mixture:
- In a bowl, combine the diced tomatoes, chopped fresh basil, minced garlic, extra virgin olive oil, and balsamic vinegar (if using).
- Season the mixture with salt and pepper to taste. Stir well to combine. Set aside to let the flavors meld together while you prepare the bread.

Toast the Bread:
- Preheat your oven to 375°F (190°C).
- Arrange the sliced baguette or Italian bread on a baking sheet in a single layer.
- Brush both sides of the bread slices lightly with olive oil.
- Optionally, rub a cut garlic clove over each bread slice for extra flavor.

Bake the Bread:
- Place the baking sheet in the preheated oven and bake the bread slices for about 8-10 minutes, or until they are golden brown and crisp. Keep an eye on them to avoid burning.

Assemble the Bruschetta:
- Once the bread slices are toasted, remove them from the oven and let them cool slightly.
- Spoon the tomato basil mixture generously onto each toasted bread slice.

Serve and Enjoy:
- Arrange the Tomato Basil Bruschetta on a serving platter.
- Serve immediately as a delicious appetizer or snack.

Tips for Serving:

- You can customize this bruschetta recipe by adding other ingredients like finely diced red onion, chopped olives, or crumbled feta cheese.
- For a twist, try grilling the bread slices instead of baking them in the oven for a smoky flavor.
- If serving the bruschetta as part of a larger meal, consider pairing it with a glass of chilled white wine or prosecco.

This Tomato Basil Bruschetta is perfect for summer gatherings, parties, or anytime you want a taste of Italy. It's fresh, vibrant, and full of Mediterranean flavors. Enjoy making and sharing this delightful appetizer with family and friends!

Buffalo Cauliflower Bites

Ingredients:

- 1 head of Cauliflower, cut into florets
- 1 cup All-purpose Flour
- 1 cup Water
- 1 teaspoon Garlic Powder
- 1 teaspoon Onion Powder
- 1/2 teaspoon Paprika
- Salt and Pepper, to taste
- 1 cup Buffalo Sauce (such as Frank's RedHot)
- 1/4 cup Unsalted Butter, melted
- Optional: Ranch or Blue Cheese dressing, for dipping

Instructions:

Preheat the Oven:
- Preheat your oven to 450°F (230°C). Line a baking sheet with parchment paper or lightly grease it with cooking spray.

Prepare the Cauliflower:
- Wash the cauliflower and cut it into bite-sized florets.

Prepare the Batter:
- In a mixing bowl, whisk together the all-purpose flour, water, garlic powder, onion powder, paprika, salt, and pepper until smooth and well-combined.

Coat the Cauliflower:
- Dip each cauliflower floret into the batter, ensuring it is well-coated.

Bake the Cauliflower:
- Place the battered cauliflower florets on the prepared baking sheet in a single layer.
- Bake for 20-25 minutes, or until the cauliflower is golden brown and crispy, flipping halfway through baking for even cooking.

Prepare the Buffalo Sauce:
- In a separate bowl, mix together the buffalo sauce and melted unsalted butter.

Coat the Cauliflower with Buffalo Sauce:
- Once the cauliflower is baked and crispy, transfer it to a large mixing bowl.
- Pour the buffalo sauce and butter mixture over the cauliflower and toss until the florets are evenly coated.

Serve:

- Transfer the buffalo cauliflower bites to a serving plate.
- Serve hot with ranch or blue cheese dressing on the side for dipping.

Tips for Serving:

- Garnish the buffalo cauliflower bites with chopped fresh parsley or chives for extra freshness and color.
- If you prefer extra spice, you can add a pinch of cayenne pepper to the batter or buffalo sauce mixture.
- Enjoy these buffalo cauliflower bites immediately while they are hot and crispy for the best texture.

Buffalo Cauliflower Bites are a flavorful and satisfying snack or appetizer that will please vegetarians and meat-eaters alike. They're perfect for game day gatherings, parties, or anytime you're craving a spicy and crunchy treat. Serve them with your favorite dipping sauce and enjoy!

Vietnamese Spring Rolls

Ingredients:

For the Spring Rolls:

- Rice paper wrappers (also known as spring roll wrappers)
- Cooked shrimp, peeled and deveined
- Rice vermicelli noodles, cooked according to package instructions and cooled
- Lettuce leaves (such as butter lettuce or Romaine), torn into small pieces
- Fresh herbs (such as Thai basil, cilantro, and mint), leaves picked
- Cucumber, julienned into thin strips
- Carrot, julienned into thin strips
- Optional: Cooked pork or tofu, sliced into thin strips

For the Dipping Sauce:

- Hoisin sauce
- Peanut butter
- Water
- Lime juice
- Soy sauce
- Sriracha sauce (optional, for a spicy kick)
- Crushed peanuts, for garnish (optional)

Instructions:

    Prepare the Ingredients:
- Cook and prepare the shrimp, rice vermicelli noodles, lettuce, herbs, cucumber, carrot, and any other fillings you are using. Ensure that all ingredients are ready and laid out for assembly.

    Soften the Rice Paper Wrappers:
- Fill a shallow dish with warm water. Dip one rice paper wrapper into the water for a few seconds until it becomes pliable and soft (be careful not to soak it for too long or it will become too sticky).

    Assemble the Spring Rolls:
- Lay the softened rice paper wrapper flat on a clean surface.
- Place a few pieces of shrimp in the center of the wrapper, followed by a small handful of cooked vermicelli noodles.

- Add torn lettuce leaves, fresh herbs, cucumber strips, carrot strips, and any other desired fillings on top of the shrimp and noodles.

Roll the Spring Rolls:
- Fold the bottom edge of the rice paper wrapper over the filling.
- Fold in the sides of the wrapper towards the center.
- Continue rolling the wrapper tightly from the bottom to the top, enclosing the filling completely.

Repeat:
- Continue assembling and rolling the remaining spring rolls with the remaining ingredients.

Make the Dipping Sauce:
- In a small bowl, whisk together hoisin sauce, peanut butter, water, lime juice, soy sauce, and sriracha sauce (if using) until smooth and well combined.

Serve:
- Arrange the Vietnamese Spring Rolls on a serving platter.
- Garnish with crushed peanuts, if desired.
- Serve with the dipping sauce on the side.

Tips for Serving:

- Serve the Vietnamese Spring Rolls immediately after assembling to prevent the rice paper wrappers from drying out.
- You can customize the fillings based on your preference and dietary restrictions. Use cooked pork, tofu, or additional vegetables as alternative fillings.
- These spring rolls are best enjoyed fresh, but you can store leftovers in an airtight container in the refrigerator for a few hours. Serve with extra dipping sauce as needed.

Vietnamese Spring Rolls are a refreshing and delicious appetizer that's perfect for gatherings and parties. They are light, healthy, and bursting with flavors. Enjoy making and savoring these delightful spring rolls with friends and family!

Greek Meatballs

Ingredients:

For the Meatballs:

- 1 pound ground beef (or a mixture of beef and lamb)
- 1 small onion, finely grated
- 2 garlic cloves, minced
- 1/2 cup breadcrumbs
- 1 egg
- 2 tablespoons chopped fresh parsley
- 1 tablespoon chopped fresh mint (optional)
- 1 teaspoon dried oregano
- 1/2 teaspoon ground cumin
- 1/2 teaspoon ground coriander
- Salt and pepper, to taste
- Olive oil, for frying

For Serving (optional):

- Tzatziki sauce
- Lemon wedges
- Chopped fresh parsley, for garnish

Instructions:

Prepare the Meatball Mixture:
- In a large mixing bowl, combine the ground beef, grated onion, minced garlic, breadcrumbs, egg, chopped parsley, chopped mint (if using), dried oregano, ground cumin, ground coriander, salt, and pepper. Mix well until all ingredients are evenly incorporated.

Shape the Meatballs:
- Take small portions of the meat mixture and roll them into meatballs, about 1 to 1.5 inches in diameter. Place the shaped meatballs on a plate or baking sheet lined with parchment paper.

Cook the Meatballs:
- Heat a few tablespoons of olive oil in a large skillet over medium-high heat.
- Add the meatballs to the skillet in batches, making sure not to overcrowd the pan. Cook the meatballs for about 3-4 minutes per side, or until they are golden brown and cooked through. Use tongs to turn the meatballs for even cooking.

Serve the Meatballs:

- Transfer the cooked meatballs to a serving platter lined with paper towels to absorb any excess oil.
- Serve the Greek meatballs hot with tzatziki sauce on the side for dipping.
- Garnish with chopped fresh parsley and lemon wedges for squeezing over the meatballs, if desired.

Tips for Serving:

- Serve the Greek Meatballs as part of a meze platter with other Greek appetizers like hummus, olives, feta cheese, and pita bread.
- Enjoy the meatballs as a main course with a side of Greek salad and crusty bread.
- Leftover meatballs can be stored in an airtight container in the refrigerator for up to 3-4 days. Reheat them gently in the microwave or oven before serving.

These Greek Meatballs are packed with Mediterranean flavors and are sure to be a hit at your next gathering or family dinner. They are easy to make and can be prepared in advance for convenience. Enjoy making and savoring these delicious meatballs with your loved ones!

Pimento Cheese Stuffed Peppers

Ingredients:

- Sweet Mini Bell Peppers (or jalapeño peppers for a spicier version)
- Pimento Cheese Spread (store-bought or homemade)
- Optional Garnish: Chopped chives, parsley, or paprika for color

Instructions:

Prepare the Peppers:
- Preheat your oven to 375°F (190°C).
- Wash the mini bell peppers and slice them in half lengthwise. Remove the seeds and membranes from inside to create little pepper boats.

Fill with Pimento Cheese:
- Spoon the pimento cheese spread into each pepper half, filling them generously.

Arrange on a Baking Sheet:
- Place the stuffed pepper halves on a baking sheet lined with parchment paper or aluminum foil for easy cleanup.

Bake:
- Bake the stuffed peppers in the preheated oven for about 12-15 minutes, or until the peppers are tender and the cheese is melted and bubbly.

Garnish and Serve:
- Remove the stuffed peppers from the oven and let them cool slightly.
- Garnish with chopped chives, parsley, or a sprinkle of paprika for color and flavor.

Serve Warm:
- Arrange the pimento cheese stuffed peppers on a serving platter.
- Serve them warm as a delicious appetizer or snack.

Tips for Variations:

- Homemade Pimento Cheese Spread: To make your own pimento cheese spread, combine shredded sharp cheddar cheese, diced pimentos, mayonnaise, cream cheese, garlic powder, and a dash of hot sauce.
- Add Some Heat: For a spicier version, use jalapeño peppers instead of mini bell peppers and fill them with the pimento cheese mixture.

Serving Suggestions:

- Serve these pimento cheese stuffed peppers as part of a party platter alongside other appetizers like crackers, sliced meats, and fresh vegetables.
- Pair them with a crisp white wine or a refreshing cocktail for a perfect appetizer pairing.

These pimento cheese stuffed peppers are easy to make and are sure to be a hit with your guests. They are a great way to enjoy the classic flavors of pimento cheese in a fun and creative way. Enjoy making and serving these delicious stuffed peppers!

Chicken Wonton Cups

Ingredients:

- Wonton Wrappers (square or round), about 24
- Cooked Chicken Breast, shredded or diced (about 1 cup)
- Bell Pepper, diced (any color)
- Green Onion, thinly sliced
- Frozen Corn, thawed (about 1/2 cup)
- Cream Cheese, softened (4 oz)
- Soy Sauce, 1 tablespoon
- Sesame Oil, 1 teaspoon
- Garlic Powder, 1/2 teaspoon
- Salt and Pepper, to taste
- Sesame Seeds, for garnish (optional)
- Chopped Fresh Cilantro or Parsley, for garnish (optional)

Instructions:

Preheat the Oven:
- Preheat your oven to 350°F (175°C). Lightly grease a mini muffin tin with cooking spray.

Prepare the Wonton Cups:
- Gently press one wonton wrapper into each cavity of the mini muffin tin, shaping them into cups. Make sure the edges of the wrappers stick up and form a cup shape. Repeat until all cavities are filled.

Make the Chicken Filling:
- In a mixing bowl, combine the cooked chicken breast, diced bell pepper, sliced green onion, thawed corn, softened cream cheese, soy sauce, sesame oil, garlic powder, salt, and pepper. Mix well until all ingredients are thoroughly combined.

Fill the Wonton Cups:
- Spoon the chicken filling mixture into each wonton cup, filling them almost to the top.

Bake the Wonton Cups:
- Place the mini muffin tin in the preheated oven and bake for 12-15 minutes, or until the edges of the wonton wrappers are golden brown and crispy.

Garnish and Serve:
- Remove the chicken wonton cups from the oven and let them cool for a few minutes in the muffin tin.
- Carefully remove the cups from the tin and arrange them on a serving platter.
- Garnish with sesame seeds and chopped fresh cilantro or parsley, if desired.

Serving Suggestions:

- Serve these chicken wonton cups warm as a delicious appetizer or party snack.

- Pair them with a dipping sauce such as sweet chili sauce, soy sauce, or hoisin sauce for extra flavor.
- Enjoy these tasty wonton cups alongside other appetizers or as part of a buffet-style spread.

These chicken wonton cups are versatile and can be customized with your favorite ingredients and seasonings. They are a crowd-pleaser and are sure to disappear quickly at any gathering. Enjoy making and sharing these delightful appetizer cups with family and friends!

Polenta Bites with Pesto and Tomato

Ingredients:

- Pre-cooked Polenta, sliced into rounds (you can find pre-cooked polenta in the refrigerated section of most grocery stores)
- Pesto Sauce, homemade or store-bought
- Cherry Tomatoes, sliced in half
- Fresh Basil Leaves, for garnish
- Olive Oil
- Salt and Pepper, to taste

Instructions:

Prepare the Polenta:
- If using pre-cooked polenta, slice it into rounds, about 1/2-inch thick. If using polenta from scratch, cook according to package instructions, spread it into a baking dish to cool and set, then cut into rounds once firm.

Cook the Polenta Rounds:
- Heat a non-stick skillet or grill pan over medium heat.
- Brush both sides of the polenta rounds with olive oil.
- Place the polenta rounds on the heated skillet and cook for 3-4 minutes on each side, or until golden brown and crispy. Remove from the skillet and set aside.

Assemble the Polenta Bites:
- Place the cooked polenta rounds on a serving platter.
- Spread a small amount of pesto sauce on each polenta round.

Add the Tomato Topping:
- Top each polenta round with a halved cherry tomato.

Garnish and Season:
- Season the polenta bites with salt and pepper to taste.
- Garnish each bite with a fresh basil leaf for added flavor and presentation.

Serve and Enjoy:
- Arrange the polenta bites on a serving platter.
- Serve them immediately as a tasty appetizer or snack.

Tips for Variations:

- Cheese: Sprinkle grated Parmesan or crumbled feta cheese on top of the pesto before adding the tomato.
- Balsamic Glaze: Drizzle a balsamic reduction over the polenta bites for extra flavor.
- Protein: Add a slice of fresh mozzarella or a grilled shrimp on top of each polenta bite for a heartier version.

Serving Suggestions:

- Serve these polenta bites with pesto and tomato as part of a party platter or alongside other appetizers.
- Pair them with a crisp white wine or a sparkling beverage for a refreshing combination.

These polenta bites with pesto and tomato are elegant, flavorful, and easy to prepare. They are perfect for entertaining and can be customized with your favorite ingredients. Enjoy making and sharing these delicious bites with family and friends!

Zucchini Fritters

Ingredients:

- 2 medium zucchini
- 1 teaspoon salt (for drawing out moisture from zucchini)
- 1/2 cup all-purpose flour
- 1/4 cup grated Parmesan cheese
- 2 cloves garlic, minced
- 2 green onions, finely chopped
- 1/4 cup fresh chopped parsley
- 2 large eggs, lightly beaten
- Salt and pepper, to taste
- Olive oil or vegetable oil, for frying
- Greek yogurt or sour cream, for serving (optional)
- Lemon wedges, for serving (optional)

Instructions:

Prepare the Zucchini:
- Grate the zucchini using a box grater or a food processor fitted with a grating attachment.
- Place the grated zucchini in a colander set over a bowl or in the sink. Sprinkle with 1 teaspoon of salt and toss to combine. Let the zucchini sit for about 10-15 minutes to release excess moisture.

Squeeze Out Excess Moisture:
- After the zucchini has released moisture, use your hands to squeeze out as much liquid as possible. You can also place the zucchini in a clean kitchen towel and wring it out to remove excess moisture.

Mix the Fritter Batter:
- In a large bowl, combine the squeezed zucchini, flour, grated Parmesan cheese, minced garlic, chopped green onions, chopped parsley, beaten eggs, salt, and pepper. Mix everything together until well combined and the mixture holds together.

Fry the Zucchini Fritters:
- Heat 2-3 tablespoons of olive oil or vegetable oil in a large skillet over medium heat.
- Scoop about 2 tablespoons of the zucchini mixture and drop it into the hot oil, pressing down lightly to flatten into a fritter shape.
- Cook the fritters in batches for about 3-4 minutes per side, or until they are golden brown and crispy. Add more oil to the skillet as needed for each batch.

Serve the Zucchini Fritters:
- Transfer the cooked fritters to a plate lined with paper towels to drain any excess oil.

- Serve the zucchini fritters warm with a dollop of Greek yogurt or sour cream on top, and lemon wedges on the side for squeezing over the fritters.

Tips for Serving:

- Zucchini fritters are delicious on their own as a snack or appetizer, but they also pair well with a fresh green salad or a side of tzatziki sauce for dipping.
- Customize the flavor by adding spices like cumin, paprika, or chili flakes to the batter.
- Leftover zucchini fritters can be stored in an airtight container in the refrigerator for up to 2-3 days. Reheat them in a toaster oven or oven until warmed through before serving.

These zucchini fritters are a wonderful way to enjoy zucchini and make a great addition to any meal. They are crispy, flavorful, and easy to make with simple ingredients. Enjoy making and savoring these delicious fritters!

Mushroom Puff Pastry Bites

Ingredients:

- 1 sheet of puff pastry, thawed (store-bought or homemade)
- 8 oz (225g) mushrooms, finely chopped (such as button mushrooms or cremini mushrooms)
- 2 cloves garlic, minced
- 2 tablespoons unsalted butter
- 1 tablespoon olive oil
- 1/4 cup finely chopped onion
- 1/4 teaspoon dried thyme
- Salt and pepper, to taste
- 1/4 cup grated Parmesan cheese (optional)
- 1 egg, beaten (for egg wash)
- Fresh parsley, chopped (for garnish, optional)

Instructions:

Prepare the Mushroom Filling:
- Heat the butter and olive oil in a skillet over medium heat.
- Add the chopped onion and cook until softened, about 2-3 minutes.
- Add the minced garlic and chopped mushrooms to the skillet. Cook, stirring occasionally, until the mushrooms release their moisture and start to brown, about 5-7 minutes.
- Stir in the dried thyme, salt, and pepper. Cook for an additional minute, then remove from heat. Allow the mushroom mixture to cool slightly.

Preheat the Oven:
- Preheat your oven to 400°F (200°C) and line a baking sheet with parchment paper.

Prepare the Puff Pastry:
- Roll out the thawed puff pastry on a lightly floured surface to a 12x12-inch square.
- Cut the puff pastry into 2-inch squares using a pizza cutter or a sharp knife.

Assemble the Mushroom Puff Pastry Bites:
- Place a small spoonful of the cooked mushroom filling in the center of each puff pastry square.
- Optionally, sprinkle some grated Parmesan cheese over the mushroom filling for added flavor.

Fold and Seal the Bites:
- Fold one corner of each puff pastry square over the filling to form a triangle.
- Use a fork to press down the edges and seal the puff pastry bites.

Brush with Egg Wash:
- Place the assembled puff pastry bites on the prepared baking sheet.
- Brush the tops of the puff pastry bites with beaten egg using a pastry brush. This will give them a golden color when baked.

Bake the Mushroom Puff Pastry Bites:
- Bake in the preheated oven for 15-18 minutes, or until the puff pastry is golden brown and puffed up.

Serve and Garnish:
- Remove the mushroom puff pastry bites from the oven and let them cool slightly on the baking sheet.
- Sprinkle with chopped fresh parsley for garnish, if desired.
- Serve the mushroom puff pastry bites warm as a delicious appetizer or snack.

Tips for Serving:

- Serve these mushroom puff pastry bites on a platter with toothpicks for easy serving at parties.
- Pair them with a dipping sauce like garlic aioli or balsamic reduction for extra flavor.
- These puff pastry bites can be made in advance and reheated in the oven before serving.

These mushroom puff pastry bites are sure to impress with their buttery, flaky crust and flavorful mushroom filling. They're perfect for any occasion and will be a hit with mushroom lovers. Enjoy making and savoring these delicious appetizers!

Avocado Shrimp Ceviche

Ingredients:

- 1 pound (450g) raw shrimp, peeled, deveined, and chopped into bite-sized pieces
- 3-4 ripe avocados, diced
- 1 cup cherry tomatoes, halved
- 1/2 red onion, finely diced
- 1 jalapeño pepper, seeded and finely chopped (optional for spice)
- 1/2 cup chopped cilantro
- Juice of 3-4 limes
- Salt and pepper, to taste
- Tortilla chips or tostadas, for serving

Instructions:

Prepare the Shrimp:
- Bring a pot of salted water to a boil. Add the chopped shrimp and cook for 2-3 minutes, until the shrimp turn pink and opaque.
- Drain the shrimp and immediately transfer them to a bowl of ice water to stop the cooking process. Drain again and pat dry with paper towels.

Combine Ingredients:
- In a large bowl, combine the cooked shrimp, diced avocados, cherry tomatoes, finely diced red onion, chopped jalapeño (if using), and chopped cilantro.

Add Lime Juice:
- Squeeze the juice of 3-4 limes over the shrimp and avocado mixture. Start with 3 limes and add more to taste.
- Season with salt and pepper, adjusting to your preference.

Mix Well:
- Gently toss all the ingredients together until well combined. Be careful not to mash the avocado.

Chill and Marinate:
- Cover the bowl with plastic wrap and refrigerate the ceviche for at least 30 minutes to allow the flavors to meld together.

Serve:
- Once chilled, give the ceviche a final stir and taste for seasoning adjustments.
- Serve the avocado shrimp ceviche in bowls or on tostadas, garnished with additional cilantro if desired.
- Serve with tortilla chips on the side for scooping up the ceviche.

Tips for Serving:

- For added flavor, you can add diced mango or pineapple to the ceviche.
- If you prefer a spicier ceviche, leave the seeds in the jalapeño or add a few dashes of hot sauce.

- Serve the avocado shrimp ceviche immediately after marinating for the best texture and flavor.

This avocado shrimp ceviche is a delightful combination of creamy avocado and zesty lime-marinated shrimp, with bursts of freshness from the vegetables. It's a perfect dish for sharing with friends and family. Enjoy making and savoring this delicious and refreshing ceviche!

Teriyaki Salmon Skewers

Ingredients:

- 1 pound (450g) salmon fillets, skinless and boneless
- 1/4 cup soy sauce
- 2 tablespoons honey
- 2 tablespoons rice vinegar
- 1 tablespoon sesame oil
- 2 cloves garlic, minced
- 1-inch piece of ginger, grated
- 2 green onions, thinly sliced
- 1 tablespoon sesame seeds
- Bamboo skewers, soaked in water (if grilling)

Instructions:

Prepare the Salmon:
- Cut the salmon fillets into cubes, about 1-inch in size. Pat them dry with paper towels and set aside.

Make the Teriyaki Marinade:
- In a bowl, whisk together the soy sauce, honey, rice vinegar, sesame oil, minced garlic, and grated ginger until well combined.

Marinate the Salmon:
- Place the salmon cubes in a shallow dish or resealable plastic bag.
- Pour the teriyaki marinade over the salmon, making sure all pieces are coated evenly. Cover or seal and refrigerate for at least 30 minutes to marinate.

Preheat the Grill or Oven:
- If using a grill, preheat it to medium-high heat. If using the oven, preheat it to 400°F (200°C). Line a baking sheet with parchment paper if baking.

Assemble the Skewers:
- Thread the marinated salmon cubes onto bamboo skewers, leaving a little space between each piece.

Cook the Skewers:
- If grilling: Place the salmon skewers on the preheated grill. Cook for about 3-4 minutes per side, or until the salmon is cooked through and slightly charred around the edges.
- If baking: Arrange the salmon skewers on the prepared baking sheet. Bake in the preheated oven for 10-12 minutes, or until the salmon is cooked through and flakes easily with a fork.

Garnish and Serve:
- Remove the cooked salmon skewers from the grill or oven.
- Sprinkle the skewers with thinly sliced green onions and sesame seeds for garnish.

Serve Warm:

- Arrange the teriyaki salmon skewers on a serving platter.
- Serve them warm as a delicious appetizer or main course.

Tips for Serving:

- Serve these teriyaki salmon skewers with steamed rice and stir-fried vegetables for a complete meal.
- Drizzle any leftover marinade over the cooked skewers for extra flavor.
- Garnish with additional chopped green onions and sesame seeds before serving.

These teriyaki salmon skewers are a crowd-pleaser and are perfect for entertaining or enjoying with family. The sweet and savory teriyaki glaze complements the tender salmon beautifully. Enjoy making and savoring these delicious skewers!

Mini Crab Tarts

Ingredients:

For the Tart Shells:

- 1 package (14 oz) frozen puff pastry, thawed
- Flour, for dusting

For the Crab Filling:

- 8 oz (about 1 cup) lump crabmeat, picked over for shells
- 4 oz cream cheese, softened
- 1/4 cup mayonnaise
- 1/4 cup grated Parmesan cheese
- 2 green onions, finely chopped
- 1 tablespoon lemon juice
- 1 teaspoon Worcestershire sauce
- 1/2 teaspoon Old Bay seasoning (or seafood seasoning of choice)
- Salt and pepper, to taste
- Fresh parsley, chopped (for garnish)

Instructions:

Preheat the Oven:
- Preheat your oven to 400°F (200°C).

Prepare the Tart Shells:
- On a lightly floured surface, roll out the thawed puff pastry to about 1/8-inch thickness.
- Using a round cookie cutter or glass, cut out circles of dough slightly larger than the wells of a mini muffin tin.
- Gently press each pastry circle into the wells of the mini muffin tin, pressing down to form a tart shell shape. Prick the bottoms of the shells with a fork to prevent puffing.

Bake the Tart Shells:
- Place the mini muffin tin with the pastry shells in the preheated oven.
- Bake for 10-12 minutes, or until the shells are golden brown and puffed. Remove from the oven and let cool slightly.

Make the Crab Filling:
- In a mixing bowl, combine the lump crabmeat, softened cream cheese, mayonnaise, grated Parmesan cheese, finely chopped green onions, lemon juice, Worcestershire sauce, Old Bay seasoning, salt, and pepper. Mix well until all ingredients are combined.

Fill the Tart Shells:
- Spoon the crab filling into the cooled pastry shells, filling each one to the top.

Bake the Mini Crab Tarts:
- Return the filled tart shells to the oven and bake for an additional 8-10 minutes, or until the filling is heated through and the tops are lightly golden.

Garnish and Serve:
- Remove the mini crab tarts from the oven and let them cool slightly in the muffin tin.
- Garnish with chopped fresh parsley.

Serve Warm:
- Carefully remove the mini crab tarts from the muffin tin and arrange them on a serving platter.
- Serve the tarts warm as a delicious appetizer.

Tips for Serving:

- Serve these mini crab tarts as part of a party spread or appetizer platter.
- Store any leftovers in an airtight container in the refrigerator and reheat gently in the oven before serving.
- Feel free to customize the filling by adding additional seasonings or herbs to suit your taste.

These mini crab tarts are rich, creamy, and full of delicious crab flavor. They are sure to be a hit at your next gathering or special occasion. Enjoy making and savoring these tasty appetizers!

Puff Pastry Pinwheels

Ingredients:

- 1 sheet of puff pastry, thawed (store-bought or homemade)
- 1/2 cup grated cheese (such as cheddar, mozzarella, or parmesan)
- 2 tablespoons finely chopped fresh herbs (such as parsley, basil, or thyme)
- 1/4 cup finely chopped cooked bacon or ham (optional)
- 1 egg, beaten (for egg wash)

Instructions:

Preheat the Oven:
- Preheat your oven to 400°F (200°C). Line a baking sheet with parchment paper.

Prepare the Puff Pastry:
- Roll out the thawed puff pastry on a lightly floured surface into a rectangle, about 10x12 inches in size.

Add Fillings:
- Sprinkle the grated cheese evenly over the surface of the puff pastry.
- Scatter the chopped fresh herbs and cooked bacon or ham (if using) over the cheese.

Roll the Pastry:
- Starting from one of the longer edges, tightly roll up the puff pastry like a jelly roll to form a log.

Slice into Pinwheels:
- Use a sharp knife to slice the log into 1/2-inch thick rounds (pinwheels). You should get about 12-14 pinwheels.

Arrange on Baking Sheet:
- Place the pinwheels on the prepared baking sheet, spacing them slightly apart.

Brush with Egg Wash:
- Brush the tops of the pinwheels with beaten egg. This will give them a golden color when baked.

Bake the Pinwheels:
- Bake in the preheated oven for 15-18 minutes, or until the pinwheels are puffed up and golden brown.

Serve Warm:
- Remove the puff pastry pinwheels from the oven and let them cool slightly on the baking sheet.

- Transfer them to a serving platter and serve warm as a delicious appetizer or snack.

Tips for Variations:

- Vegetarian Option: Skip the bacon or ham and use additional cheese and vegetables like diced bell peppers, spinach, or caramelized onions.
- Sweet Version: Instead of savory fillings, try filling the puff pastry with Nutella, cinnamon sugar, or fruit preserves for a sweet treat.

Serving Suggestions:

- Serve these puff pastry pinwheels as appetizers at parties or gatherings.
- Enjoy them as a quick snack or light meal alongside a salad or soup.
- Customize the fillings based on your preferences and experiment with different flavor combinations.

These puff pastry pinwheels are versatile, easy to make, and always a crowd-pleaser. Feel free to get creative with the fillings and enjoy these delicious savory pastries!

Olive and Cheese Skewers

Ingredients:

- Assorted olives (such as green, black, or Kalamata), pitted
- Cheese cubes (such as mozzarella, cheddar, or provolone)
- Cherry tomatoes
- Fresh basil leaves (optional)
- Wooden skewers or toothpicks

Instructions:

   Prepare the Ingredients:
   - If using wooden skewers, soak them in water for about 15-20 minutes to prevent them from splintering.
   - Gather your olives, cheese cubes, cherry tomatoes, and fresh basil leaves (if using).

   Assemble the Skewers:
   - Start by threading one olive onto the skewer.
   - Follow with a cheese cube, then a cherry tomato.
   - If using fresh basil leaves, fold a leaf and add it next.
   - Repeat the pattern until the skewer is filled, leaving a little space at the top for easy handling.

   Repeat and Customize:
   - Continue assembling the olive and cheese skewers until you've used up all your ingredients.
   - Feel free to customize the skewers with different combinations of olives, cheese, and tomatoes.

   Serve and Enjoy:
   - Arrange the olive and cheese skewers on a serving platter.
   - Serve them as appetizers or snacks at your gathering or party.

Tips for Serving:

- Add variety by using different types of olives such as green, black, or marinated varieties.
- Experiment with different cheeses like mozzarella, cheddar, provolone, or feta for a range of flavors.
- Drizzle the skewers with a little balsamic glaze or olive oil before serving for extra flavor.

- Serve the skewers alongside a dipping sauce like pesto or hummus for added enjoyment.

Olive and cheese skewers are versatile, quick to assemble, and always a hit with guests. They offer a wonderful combination of flavors and textures that everyone will enjoy. Feel free to get creative and make these appetizers your own!

www.ingramcontent.com/pod-product-compliance
Lightning Source LLC
LaVergne TN
LVHW061943070526
838199LV00060B/3943